ManageFirst
PROGRAM™

NRAEF ManageFirst
Menu Marketing and Management

Competency Guide

PEARSON
Prentice
Hall

Upper Saddle River, New Jersey 07458

National Restaurant Association
EDUCATIONAL FOUNDATION

Disclaimer

Published by Pearson Prentice Hall, 1 Lake Street, Upper Saddle River, NJ 07458

The information presented in this book has been compiled from sources and documents believed to be reliable and represents the best professional judgment of the National Restaurant Association Educational Foundation. The accuracy of the information presented, however, is not guaranteed, nor is any responsibility assumed or implied, by the National Restaurant Association Educational Foundation for any damage or loss resulting from inaccuracies or omissions.

Laws may vary greatly by city, county, or state. This book is not intended to provide legal advice or establish standards of reasonable behavior. Operators are urged to use the advice and guidance of legal counsel.

Requests for permission to use or reproduce material from this book should be directed to:

Copyright Permissions
National Restaurant Association Educational Foundation
175 West Jackson Boulevard, Suite 1500
Chicago, IL 60604
312.715.1010
Fax 312.566.9729
Email: permissions@nraef.org

Visit www.nraef.org for information on other National Restaurant Association Educational Foundation products and programs.

The National Restaurant Association Educational Foundation prohibits discrimination in all its programs and activities on the basis of race, color, national origin, gender, religion, age, disability, political beliefs, sexual orientation, or marital or family status.

The National Restaurant Association Educational Foundation is an equal opportunity employer.

NRAEF ManageFirst Program™, ServSafe®, and ServSafe Alcohol™ are either trademarks or registered trademarks of the National Restaurant Association Educational Foundation.

ISBN 0-13-222201-9

Printed in the U.S.A.

10 9 8 7 6 5 4 3 2 1

Table of Contents

A Message from the National Restaurant Association Educational Foundation

The National Restaurant Association Educational Foundation (NRAEF) is a not-for-profit organization dedicated to fulfilling the educational mission of the National Restaurant Association. We focus on helping the restaurant and foodservice industry address its risk management, recruitment, and retention challenges.

As the nation's largest private-sector employer, the restaurant, hospitality, and foodservice industry is the cornerstone of the American economy, of career-and-employment opportunities, and of local communities. The total economic impact of the restaurant industry is astounding—representing approximately 10 percent of the U.S. gross domestic product. At the NRAEF, we are focused on enhancing this position by providing the valuable tools and resources needed to educate our current and future professionals.

For more information on the NRAEF, please visit our Web site at *www.nraef.org.*

What is the NRAEF ManageFirst Program?

The NRAEF ManageFirst Program is a management-training certificate program that exemplifies our commitment to developing materials by the industry, for the industry. The program's most powerful strength is that it is based on a set of competencies defined by the restaurant, foodservice, and hospitality industry as critical for success.

NRAEF ManageFirst Program Components

The NRAEF ManageFirst Program includes a set of competency guides, exams, instructor resources, certificates, a new credential, and support activities and services. By participating in the program, you are demonstrating your commitment to becoming a highly qualified professional either preparing to begin or to advance your career in the restaurant, hospitality, and foodservice industry.

The competency guides cover the range of topics listed in the chart at right.

Competency Guide/Exam Topics

NRAEF ManageFirst Core Credential Topics

Hospitality and Restaurant Management

Controlling Foodservice Costs

Human Resources Management and Supervision

ServSafe® Food Safety

NRAEF ManageFirst Foundation Topics

Managerial Accounting

Inventory and Purchasing

Customer Service

Food Production

Menu Marketing and Management

Restaurant Marketing

Nutrition

ServSafe Alcohol™ Responsible Alcohol Service

Within the guides, you will find the essential content for the topic as defined by industry, as well as learning activities, assessments, case studies, suggested field projects, professional profiles, and testimonials. You will also find an answer sheet for an NRAEF exam written specifically for each topic. The exam can be administered either online or in a paper and pencil format, and it will be proctored. Upon successfully passing the exam, you will be furnished by the NRAEF with a customized certificate. The certificate is a lasting recognition of your accomplishment and a signal to the industry that you have mastered the competency covered within the particular topic.

To earn the NRAEF's new credential, you will be required to pass four core exams and one foundation exam (to be chosen from the remaining program topics) and to document your work experience in the restaurant and foodservice industry. Earning the NRAEF credential is a significant accomplishment.

We applaud you as you begin or advance your career in the restaurant, hospitality, and foodservice industry. Visit www.nraef.org to learn about additional career-building resources offered by the NRAEF, including scholarships for college students enrolled in relevant industry programs.

NRAEF ManageFirst Program Ordering Information

Review copies or support materials:
FACULTY FIELD SERVICES
800.526.0485

Domestic orders and inquiries:
PEARSON CUSTOMER SERVICE
Tel: 800.922.0579
www.prenhall.com

International orders and inquiries:
U.S. EXPORT SALES OFFICE
Pearson Education International Customer Service Group
200 Old Tappan Road
Old Tappan, NJ 07675 USA
Tel: 201.767.5021
Fax: 201.767.5625

For corporate, government and special sales (consultants, corporations, training centers, VARs, and corporate resellers) orders and inquiries:
PEARSON CORPORATE SALES
Phone: 317.428.3411
Fax: 317.428.3343
Email: managefirst@prenhall.com

For additional information regarding other Prentice Hall publications, instructor and student support materials, locating your sales representative and much more, please visit www.prenhall.com/managefirst.

Acknowledgements

The National Restaurant Association Educational Foundation is grateful for the expertise and guidance of our many advisors, subject matter experts, reviewers, and other contributors.

We are pleased to thank the following people for their time, effort, and dedication to this program.

Ernest Boger

Robert Bosselman

Jerald Chesser

Cynthia Deale

Fred DeMicco

John Drysdale

Gene Fritz

John Gescheidle

Thomas Hamilton

John Hart

Thomas Kaltenecker

Ray Kavanaugh

John Kidwell

Carol Kizer

Fred Mayo

Cynthia Mayo

Patrick Moreo

Robert O'Halloran

Brian O'Malley

Terrence Pappas

James Perry

William N. Reynolds

Rosenthal Group

Mokie Steiskal

Karl Titz

Terry Umbreit

Deanne Williams

Mike Zema

Features of the NRAEF ManageFirst Competency Guides

We have designed the NRAEF ManageFirst Competency Guides to enhance your ability to learn and retain important information that is critical to this restaurant and foodservice industry function. Here are the key features you will find within this guide.

Beginning Each Guide

Tuning In to You

When you open an NRAEF ManageFirst Competency Guide for the first time, you might ask yourself: Why do I need to know about this topic? Every topic of these guides involves key information you will be need as you manage a restaurant or foodservice operation. Located in the front of each review guide, "Tuning In to You" is a brief synopsis that illustrates some of the reasons the information contained throughout that particular guide is important to you. It exemplifies real-life scenarios that you will face as a manager and how the concepts in the book will help you in your career.

Professional Profile

This is your opportunity to meet a professional who is currently working in the field associated with a competency guide's topic. This person's story will help you gain insight into the responsibilities related to his or her position, as well as the training and educational history linked to it. You will also see the daily and cumulative impact this position has on an operation, and receive advice from a person who has successfully met the challenges of being a manager.

Beginning Each Chapter

Inside This Chapter

Chapter content is organized under these major headings.

Learning Objectives

Learning objectives identify what you should be able to do after completing each chapter. These objectives are linked to the required tasks a manager must be able to perform in relation to the function discussed in the competency guide.

Test Your Knowledge

Each chapter begins with some True or False questions designed to test your prior knowledge of some of the concepts presented in the chapter. The answers to these questions, as well as the concepts behind them, can be found within the chapter—see the page reference after each question.

Key Terms

These terms are important for thorough understanding of the chapter's content. They are highlighted throughout the chapter, where they are explicitly defined or their meaning is made clear within the paragraphs in which they appear.

Throughout Each Chapter

Exhibits

Exhibits are placed throughout each chapter to visually reinforce the key concepts presented in the text. Types of exhibits include charts, tables, photographs, and illustrations.

Think About It...

These thought-provoking sidebars reveal supportive information about the section they appear beside.

Activities

Apply what you have learned throughout the chapter by completing the various activities in the text. The activities have been designed to give you additional practice and better understanding of the concepts addressed in the learning objectives. Types of activities include case studies, role-plays, and problem solving, among others.

Exhibit

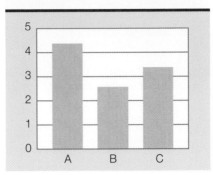

Exhibits are visuals that will help you learn about key concepts.

Activity

Activity

Types of activities you will complete include case studies, role-plays, and problem solving, among others.

Think About It...

Consider these supplemental insights as you read through a chapter.

At the End of Each Chapter

Review Your Learning

These multiple-choice or open- or close-ended questions or problems are designed to test your knowledge of the concepts presented in the chapter. These questions have been aligned with the objectives and should provide you with an opportunity to practice or apply the content that supports these objectives. If you have difficulty answering them, you should review the content further.

At the End of the Guide

Field Project

This real-world project gives you the valuable opportunity to apply many of the concepts you will learn in a competency guide. You will interact with industry practitioners, enhance your knowledge, and research, apply, analyze, evaluate, and report on your findings. It will provide you with an in-depth "reality check" of the policies and practices of this management function.

Tuning In to You

Have you ever gone to your favorite restaurant and been handed a menu that looked different from the one you were used to? What was your first reaction? Most people see an updated menu at their favorite place and experience a moment of panic—"Are my favorite items still available? Why was the menu changed? What was changed? I liked it just fine the way it was."

Chances are, most of the changes made to the menu will not make much difference to you, a regular customer. The layout might have been updated, perhaps the prices, too. Some items might have been eliminated, but certainly not the most popular or high-profit items. There might be new items that are being introduced. Some items might even be getting "star treatment" as house specialties. Whatever the changes are, they were most likely planned and evaluated well in advance of implementing the new menu.

The menu of a foodservice operation is a very critical element of its success. Changes to the menu can markedly increase sales if done well, or decrease sales if done poorly. There is plenty to consider in planning an effective menu, from the operation's marketing environment, its competition, brand image, and availability of foods, to the skills and capabilities of its kitchen and dining staff. Though it may seem unmanageable, all of these different aspects of the business can be brought together to help plan out exactly what should be on a menu.

The menu is also the most important sales and marketing tool available to a restaurant. Both the design and layout are key to making items appeal to customers, provide the information they need, guide them to the most profitable items, and produce profits for a foodservice operation. The psychology of design is a proven factor influencing what customers order.

One goal of a good menu is to create interest—or even excitement—for customers while meeting their individual tastes and nutritional needs. You have to consider nutrition, customers' indulgence, dietary restriction, price, convenience, value, and merchandising. Juggling these factors—along with cooking methods, food cost, competitive pricing, and food labeling requirements—to deliver high quality menu items is an art.

You can see that menu management involves more than creating a list of randomly selected food and beverage items. It involves psychology—in fact, several kinds. It also involves math, the knowledge of food preparation processes, equipment, and tools, and the knowledge of purchasing food ingredients. There is a lot depending on you to manage and market your operation's menus well. Once you learn these important basics, you too will be able to plan and update a menu that will result in happy customers and happy owners.

Professional Profile
Your opportunity to meet someone working in the field

Thom Coffman

Proprietor
The Clarmont
Columbus, Ohio

What do a train engineer and an independent owner/operator of a restaurant have in common? The answer is: being available around the clock. And I should know, since I have been both a train engineer and a restaurant owner.

My current duties as a restaurant proprietor include the entire responsibility for the menu—with a little help from my chef, who assists with some recipe development (I have also been known to take a turn in the kitchen myself). In addition, I am responsible for purchasing, operations management, human resources management, and customer relations, as well as busing tables, assisting servers where needed, and solving customer problems.

I came to Columbus, Ohio, in the early 1980s, both to make a career change and to learn all I could about the restaurant business. I enrolled in the Hospitality Management program at Columbus State Community College and graduated in 1985. While attending school full-time, I started working in a local restaurant, where my work ranged from kitchen prep to busing tables to serving, and everything in between. After graduation, I continued to work in a variety of fine-dining venues in downtown Columbus. In 1996, I had the opportunity to purchase The Clarmont, a well-established fine-dining restaurant that originally opened in 1947; it has been in business far longer than any other "white-tablecloth" restaurant in Columbus. It is located at 684 South High Street, tucked between the Brewery District and German Village.

The Clarmont is a 155-seat restaurant with a bar. Breakfast, lunch, and dinner are served Monday through Saturday, and dinner is served on Sunday. The restaurant normally opens at 4 p.m. on Sunday, but will open early for special occasions such as Mother's Day. There are three separate menus and a wine list used in this operation. Although we do not offer a children's menu, there are several dishes suitable for younger guests. My serving staff, some of whom have been there for over twenty years, have been trained to explain the options available for children. We do no have a set dessert menu, so that the chef can have some freedom to prepare different desserts daily. The desserts are sold as well through server suggestion.

The restaurant serves traditional breakfast items, with an average check of about $6.50. The prices of the breakfast menu items are based a little more on food cost than the prices of other meals. The lunch menu, with an average check of about $11.50, offers some of the dinner entrées—in particular, steaks—however, we really sell a lot of sandwiches during lunch. We try to "hide" the steaks, both on the lunch and dinner menus, because they aren't as profitable as they used to be.

The dinner menu includes Clarmont Classics, such as The Classic Tenderloin, Rack of Lamb, and Lamb Osso Bucco, as well as two pork dishes, a veal chop, and two fish items. We also highlight Special Features near the top right-hand corner of the menu, and these include: four special seafood items, calves liver, pork chops, barbequed ribs, duckling, roasted chicken, two more seafood entrées, and Kobe chopped beef steak. Then we offer several steaks, followed by the Prime Rib of Beef, which is highlighted in a box on the menu. The dinner check average is about $22.15.

Over the years, I have found the price point above which my customers will not go. The current highest menu price is $29.50 for a twelve-ounce filet mignon, and few will pay that price; none of my customers would pay $35.00 for a steak. Pricing methodology for the luncheon and dinner entrées is based more on knowing the operation's daily expenses, the average customer count, and what the customers are willing to pay. The reason why the steaks, a Clarmont tradition, are placed in less obvious places on the lunch and dinner menus is because when the cost of beef went up, I was a little slow to react to this cost increase and it hurt the operation's cash flow. The pricing structure at the time was not providing us with enough gross profit to pay expenses and retain profit. So then I raised the prices somewhat and rearranged the menu to feature other items.

I make the effort to really know my customers. At breakfast, we serve business people and state and local government officials. Our lunch crowd includes many of the local real estate developers, realtors, and contractors. Our dinner crowd includes many local regulars, and business is really good when there are theater events in town.

My advice for the new menu planner is to pay attention to textbooks written about menus, gain industry experience, use what you learn in school, read current articles from professional and trade periodicals, and adapt to customers. I change the menu about twice a year, in the spring and fall. The changes are based on customer requests and sales analysis, as well as my own ideas—I try to eat in another individually owned and operated restaurant on a weekly basis, for fun and for new ideas.

I recently completed a term as president of the Central Ohio Restaurant Association and have just assumed responsibilities as the secretary/treasurer of the Ohio Restaurant Association. I learn quite a bit from other association members, and I enjoy contributing to the industry as well.

Factors That Impact Menu Item Selection

1

Inside This Chapter
- Marketing Environment
- Selecting Menu Items
- Changing a Menu
- Internal Operational Concerns When Choosing New Items

After completing this chapter, you should be able to:
- Define foodservice terms related to menus.
- Identify elements of the marketing environment.
- List factors that impact menu item selection.
- Select menu items.
- Discuss the impact of internal concerns when selecting menu items.

Test Your Knowledge

1. **True or False:** It does not matter what the competition has on its menu; you should put on your menu what you can sell profitably. *(See pp. 3–4.)*

2. **True or False:** The capability of the kitchen staff should not be considered when adding items that customers want to the menu; you can always train them or hire new staff. *(See p. 12.)*

3. **True or False:** Providing healthy menu choices is a long-range trend, not a fad; it is not going away. *(See p. 5.)*

4. **True or False:** The best way to have a successful menu and a profitable business is for menu planners to meet the needs of all kinds of customers. *(See p. 3.)*

5. **True or False:** To develop a successful menu, the planner should start by listing all the appetizers they would like to have appear and then continue on through each menu category in the same way. *(See p. 9.)*

Key Terms

Brand	Price point
Contribution margin	Target customers
Direct competitors	Target market
Indirect competitors	Target profit margin
Operational execution	Trademark

Think About It...

Why do you frequent one restaurant and not another? How much of your reason is related to the menu items and prices?

Introduction

There is more to selecting menu items than just choosing your favorite types of food. Of course, the most important consideration in creating a menu is the customer. You first must determine who your customers are, what they want, and how to attract them. To profitably serve them, you must also consider your operation's target margins, sales potential, and price points. Additionally, you must look at the marketing environment in which a restaurant operates, including competition, pricing, consumer and industry trends, and brand image. The availability of food items and the skills and capabilities of the kitchen and dining staff are important too, as are operating efficiency, staff capability, and equipment. Taking these factors into account, you must then determine how an operation can effectively produce the menu items it wants to offer.

Marketing Environment

To begin planning a menu, you must consider a variety of external factors that affect it. This section discusses some of the marketing concerns you must be aware of when the menu is first developed. However, because the marketing environment changes over time, you should also continuously monitor the environment and adjust accordingly.

A menu for a restaurant must be planned with an understanding of the marketing environment in which it exists. There are several environmental aspects to consider:

- Target market
- Competition
- Consumer trends
- Restaurant and foodservice industry trends

Exhibit 1a

Target customers

Target Market

An important first step in designing a menu is to identify the customers that the restaurant and its menu are designed to serve. This group can be called the target market or target customers—a group of people with similar characteristics and similar demands of the marketplace. (See *Exhibit 1a*.) This group can be identified using customer demographic information.

A large part of a restaurant's success rests on its management's ability to target a large enough group within a reasonable distance from the restaurant's location. The particular characteristics of such a group are important when researching the target market. Factors to be considered include how often they dine out, the price they are willing to pay, the ambience and type of service they want, the types of food they enjoy, and their proximity to the restaurant or foodservice operation.

Competition

Another important factor to consider is the existence of other restaurants competing for similar customers. Once the competition has been identified, it is important to assess the menu items offered by these restaurants. (See *Exhibit 1b* on the next page.) If they are successful operations, they probably have a good idea of their target market's menu item preferences and pricing expectations. Your establishment might find it useful to provide similar offerings.

Exhibit 1b

Example of two restaurants vying for the same customers

However, to capture some of this target market, you must consider how the menu being planned will serve this customer better. One way to attract the customer is to offer a unique or signature menu item. These signature items should be something that suits the character of the operation and comfortably fits with the rest of the menu. Another way to attract customers is to provide menu items similar to those offered by the competition, while setting and meeting higher standards for preparation, presentation, and service.

When examining the competition's menu, pricing is also important. Remember that one of the reasons customers belong to a specified target market is the price they are willing to pay for the perceived value of the food and service they receive. To be competitive, prices on the planned menu should be similar to those of the competition. However, if the competition is an independently owned restaurant, it will be difficult to know how successful it really is. You must use sound business and pricing practices when pricing competitively; this will provide the restaurant with enough income to cover operating costs and meet the target profit margin. (More about this will be discussed in Chapter 4.)

Activity

Beat the Competition

You plan the menu for Chuck's Chuckwagon, a family restaurant featuring Western menu items with standard family-type menu offerings. Competition has increased from new and existing restaurants in your market area, including independently owned operations and members of a national chain. Their advertising is effective, especially that of the national chain restaurants. You have consequently suffered a loss of business. Although the situation is challenging, you are determined not to give up, and you make a commitment to take on your competition and win back your customers.

What can you do to stand out and to foil the competition? Divide into teams and prepare a list of ideas on a separate piece of paper to draw new and old customers into your restaurant and turn the tables on your competitors. The team with the longest list wins the most customers.

Exhibit 1c

Trend or Fad?

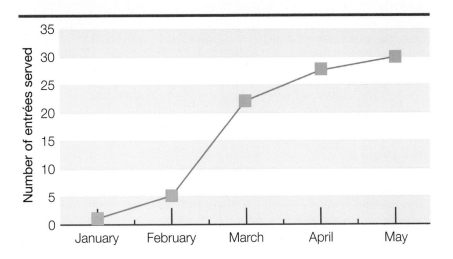

There is not enough information to decide if interest in this entrée is a trend or a fad.

Consumer Trends

Consumer trends affect the market environment for which a menu is planned. A desire for healthier eating appears to be a long-term trend rather than a fad. (See Chapter 2 for more information about offering healthy menu items.) Some diets are considered fads, but others are trends. For example, some consumers once considered "low-fat" and "low-carb" diets healthy, but both concepts are not as popular now as they used to be.

A trend grows and may level off, but its related level of sales is held for a long period of time. A fad grows rapidly but then peaks and declines quickly to zero. It is important to distinguish between a fad and a trend because changing a menu may involve several things:

- Assessing the target customers' interest in the trend

- Investing in equipment not currently owned to properly prepare more healthy food items

- Testing and modifying recipes

- Retraining cooks to prepare healthier food items

- Redesigning the menu itself

Mistakenly treating a fad as a long-term trend may result in many changes that have to be changed back when the fad is over. (See *Exhibit 1c.*)

A long-term trend that does appear to be sustaining interest is the popularity of Asian cuisine; this is actually a subcategory of the healthy eating trend because Asian fare is seen as more healthy. Adding Asian food items to a menu should be done only after careful consideration since it has a strong impact on the menu and its delivery. This is because Asian food preparation requires very different equipment and skills than those used in most Western restaurants. Sometimes adding a new type of food like Asian food does not fit the menu, the restaurant décor, the capabilities of the staff, and the like. Moreover, even though the popularity of

Asian fare may be a long-term trend, the restaurant's target market may not be interested.

Another consumer trend is that of families eating out more because of a lack or perceived lack of time. This trend has been growing for some time and does not appear to be slowing. This trend affects menus in three ways:

- Need for children's items, portions, prices, and menus

- Need for changes or additions to the décor, such as high chairs and other child-oriented items

- Need for menu items (meals) that can be heated and consumed at home

Exhibit 1d

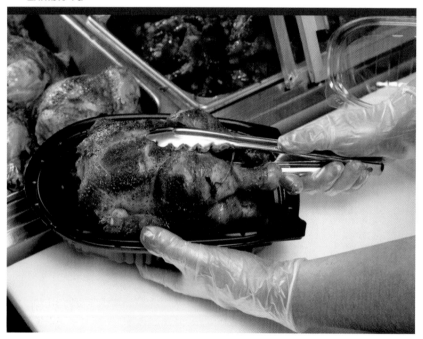

Food prepared and served in grocery stores offers additional competition for restaurants.

Restaurant and Foodservice Industry Trends

One restaurant and foodservice industry trend is increased competition. Restaurants are encountering additional **direct competitors**—other restaurants in the same market targeting the same customers. Restaurants are also facing **indirect competitors,** such as grocery stores serving food and complete meals that are ready to eat. (See *Exhibit 1d.*) In the face of such competition as well as an uncertain economy, restaurants are more carefully pricing menu offerings to continue to attract business.

When profits are tight due to intense competition, controlling costs is critical. Controlling purchasing and production practices is very important to controlling costs. Paying more attention to such controls is necessary to remain profitable. Also, restaurants are more likely to offer substitutions at no added cost to satisfy customers' wants and needs.

Another industry trend is to provide a variety of menu choices to customers to maintain their interest in the menu and the restaurant. Establishments must learn as much as possible about customers to continue to meet their needs, even as they change.

Brand Image

One factor that sets a restaurant apart from the competition is its brand image. A **brand** encompasses those things used to identify the goods and services offered by a restaurant and to differentiate the establishment from its competitors. In other words, the brand defines what the restaurant does and provides the heart and backbone of the operation's mission statement. Creating a brand image is an important part of the success of a restaurant operation because it communicates to the customer, as well as to employees, the restaurant's mission and the organization's values.

Exhibit 1e

A strong, well-defined brand is important for generating customer loyalty and visibility in the community.

A brand's purpose is to create an image in consumers' minds that signifies a specific, desired perception of value for price, also known as positioning. A strong, well-defined brand is important for generating customer loyalty and visibility in the community. The physical brand may include a name, logo, symbol, or design. (See *Exhibit 1e.*) In addition to these physical aspects of a brand, the brand image may be reinforced by the restaurant's exterior and interior décor, its type of service, its level of quality, the look of the menu, the type of menu items offered, the menu price categories, and product consistency.

Because a brand is reinforced through the menu, the brand can be tarnished if (1) the menu components do not support each other, (2) the menu components do not support the other implementations of the brand, or (3) the value perceived by the customer does not match what the restaurant offers. Therefore, managing the brand aspect of a menu and the menu items is extremely important to the success of a restaurant or foodservice operation. Additionally, some brands are given legal protection through the use of a **trademark.** The trademark protects the brand name or symbol from use by others.

Operational Execution

For a restaurant to be successful, components of the operation must work together. A menu item selected by a customer should be prepared and served well, match the description on the menu, provide value for the price, and consequently, support the brand image. **Operational execution** is the term used to describe how all parts of the restaurant work together to provide the customer with a positive dining experience. If the carefully planned menu items cannot be purchased by the buyer, prepared well by the cooks, and served by the service personnel, and the customer does not receive value for the price, then the menu has not been executed well. Menu planning goes beyond what is printed on the paper and offered to the customer; a successful restaurant menu planner must consider all operational components.

Once these fundamental decisions have been made, it is time to select the actual items for the menu.

Selecting Menu Items

The menu development process includes the identification and selection of menu items to place on the menu. This process must consider the target market—customers whom the foodservice operation intends to serve. However, the basic method is the same regardless of the target market, and there is a definite sequence of steps that should be followed to determine a restaurant's menu.

Size of the Menu

The first thing to be decided is the size of the menu. Is it to be a large, extensive menu or a more limited menu? Many restaurant operators try to maintain a balance between the two.

The advantage of a limited menu is the savings in the amount of equipment, inventory and storage space needed. A limited menu also requires less skilled labor because production is simpler. In general, it is easier to control costs and quality with a limited menu. On the other hand, it is then typically difficult to attract a large customer base.

Generally, a more extensive menu can attract a greater number of customers and can encourage regular customers to return because of the larger variety of choices available. An extensive menu, however, requires larger inventory, more storage, more highly skilled labor, more equipment, and a larger production space. Controlling costs and quality are also more of a challenge.

Exhibit 1f

Common Menu Categories

1. Appetizers
2. Soups
3. Salads
4. Sandwiches
5. Signature entrées
6. Entrées
7. Side dishes
8. Desserts
9. Beverages
10. Alcoholic beverages

Think About It...

A restaurant manager is considering putting several cuts and sizes of steak on the menu at one-dollar price differences, ranging from $11.95 to $21.95. Would you be able to detect a different value for each one? Would you be willing to pay $21.95 for the most expensive steak?

Categories of Food

Once the general size of the menu is determined, the categories of food items to offer should be selected. This involves deciding whether the menu will offer appetizers, soups, salads, sandwiches, entrées, desserts, etc. (See *Exhibit 1f.*) Every restaurant does not have to offer food in every category. Be cautious in selecting categories to offer because more categories mean more menu items to prepare.

Breadth of Categories

After the categories of menu offerings have been selected, the number of choices in each category should be decided. In this step, consideration is given to the specific kinds of entrées, salads, desserts, etc., that will be offered. For example, a menu planner might decide that the entrées should include two poultry items, four beef items, two pork items, three seafood items, and two pasta items.

Selecting the Price Point

A major influence on the menu items to be included is consideration of price points. A price point is the dollar amount customers are willing to pay for menu items during a specific meal period. The price point for breakfast items might be lower than the price point a customer is willing to pay for dinner in the same restaurant.

An alternate way to describe the price point is the maximum dollar amount a customer is willing to pay for a menu item while considering the value the customer places on the item. If the menu items are priced too high, then customers will choose to dine elsewhere. If the menu items are priced too low, then profits may be limited. Additionally, consideration must be given to the cost of producing the selected menu items and whether or not the target customers are willing to pay the price necessary to cover the costs.

Select Specific Menu Items in Each Category

Now that the breadth and price point of each category has been determined, you can select the specific menu items for each category. To do this, you must consider all of the following:

■ Time of day and the items commonly served at that time

■ Cuts of meat, fish, and poultry available within the restaurant's cost parameters

■ Equipment and other capabilities of the kitchen

■ Skills and motivations of the cooking and serving staff

- Preparation techniques available for use

- Variety of the menu items in regard to color, texture, and flavor

- Nutritional value of the menu items

- Food tastes and interests of the clientele as determined by market research or experience

- Reputation and brand of the restaurant

- Desires of the customers for speed and convenience versus atmosphere and luxury

Changing a Menu

After the menu has been in use for a while, the decision to change it might be made. Questions to be answered in making a change are:

- Should a menu item be dropped?

- Does the new menu item have sales potential?

- Will the new item fit with the established menu in terms of production, price point, and brand?

Exhibit 1g

TRY OUR
NEWEST ITEM

CHICKEN PAPRIKASH

A DELIGHTFUL BLEND
OF HUNGARIAN SPICES
IN A RICH SAVORY
SAUCE OVER CHICKEN
AND EGG NOODLES

Table tent cards are an easy way to feature a new menu item.

Testing New Items

If the proposed item can be produced within your operation efficiently within cost parameters and it fits your brand, then it should be tested for sales potential. An important step in the process is to try the new item out on the staff. If the servers like it, they will sell it. If the cooks like it and can produce it efficiently, they will prepare it to the best of their ability. Following that, the menu item should be offered to guests as a special to determine their reaction to it. Ask for customer comments either verbally or through a feedback card, and check how much that was left on the plates brought back to the kitchen. The new item should be tested on customers more than once because different customers have different likes and dislikes.

If 60 percent or more of the customers say they like it and would order it again, it can be considered a good addition to the menu. Once the new item is on the menu, promote sales of the new item by listing it on table tent cards (see *Exhibit 1g*), and have servers actively sell it by suggesting it to their customers. You could also provide servers with an incentive to sell the new item.

Pricing New Items

Another consideration given to placing items on the menu is whether they can be priced at a level high enough to produce the desired **target profit margins**—the net profit remaining to the investors and owners after all costs and business taxes have been paid. Each item on the menu must yield a profit margin at or above the target profit margin sought by the restaurant.

Every restaurant has its structure of fixed, variable, and semivariable costs for offering food to the public, and every restaurant has competition affecting the prices that it can charge. Some items can be produced and sold in such a way that enough profit is realized. That is not, however, always the case. Even though a new menu item is right for the restaurant and liked by customers, it might not be producible at a cost low enough or sold at a price high enough to make a profit for the restaurant.

Here is an example of how evaluating a new menu item's profitability works: Maria's Trattoria wants to add Chicken Vesuvio to its menu. A complete serving with side dishes can be produced for a food and labor cost of $11.25. Overhead, such as rent and utilities, adds 45 percent of this cost, or $5.06, for a total of $16.31. Maria's target profit margin is 10 percent of the combination of food preparation cost and overhead, or 10 percent of $16.31, which is $1.63. This brings the total selling price to $16.31 + $1.63, which equals $17.94. The item would then be placed on the menu at the psychologically attractive price of $17.95. Unfortunately, the nearby Cucina Italiano sells Chicken Vesuvio for $16.95. Maria's could match that price, but then there would be too little profit. So Maria's cannot afford to put Chicken Vesuvio on its menu.

The target profit margin—or simply profit—is usually established as a percentage of sales, such as 5 percent or 10 percent. The target profit margin for Maria's Trattoria is 9 percent of sales (9 percent of Chicken Vesuvio's price of $17.95 equals $1.62, which is close to 10 percent of its costs, or $1.63). The target profit margin should be established with the return on investment as a primary consideration. It can be achieved only through catering to the target market, through menu pricing, and through operational control.

Internal Operational Concerns When Choosing New Items

One of the major challenges presented to menu planners is to maintain the currency and popularity of menu offerings as trends and customer demands change. Any change in menu impacts (1) the flow of production in the kitchen, (2) the mix of menu items sold, (3) the purchasing and storage function, (4) the equipment needed, (5) the profitability of the menu possibly, the flow of service

Effect on Menu Mix

A new menu item might impact the frequency with which other menu items are ordered. A change in menu mix could influence pre-preparation of food items as well as the actual cooking of the items—the whole dynamic of the kitchen operation.

Effect on Profit

A change in menu mix might also impact the profitability of the operation. The new item might not provide as much of its price towards profit—its **contribution margin,** or the difference between selling price and food cost. One part of the contribution is fixed expenses; the other is profit. If the contribution margin is too low, profit takes the hit. Or, the new item might attract customers away from the high-profit items. In both cases, the net profit would be reduced.

Exhibit 1h

You must have enough kitchen staff to support the items on your menu.

Effect on the Kitchen

Consideration should be given to the available capacity of the kitchen production station that will be responsible for producing the new item. (See *Exhibit 1h.*) If the kitchen staff is already overloaded at the sauté station, for instance, adding a new sauté item to the menu will have a negative impact on production. Or if the new item requires more production resources, all other work will have to slow down to accommodate.

Effects on Ingredients

The availability of ingredients for the new menu item must be considered. The purchaser will need to find a source of the ingredients. The storage manager will have to find a place in the storage facility for the new item. If it requires totally new ingredients, the size and expense of inventory will increase.

Effect on Equipment

A major change in the menu offerings may require the purchase and installation of a new piece of equipment to prepare the item. In addition to the budget impact of the new equipment purchase, it is often a challenge finding the new equipment an appropriate place in the production line. Many pieces of cooking equipment need electricity, gas, water, or drainpipe connections; some require several connections. A hood to remove smoke and odors from a new piece of equipment may be necessary. The addition of a menu item may quite literally rearrange the whole kitchen.

Effect on Production Staff

A change in menu may require retraining of the production and service staff. If the menu items are too difficult to produce, cooks may become frustrated or less motivated to perform their duties well. If the menu items are too simple, they may become bored. Because labor is a large cost of producing the menu, it is important to match the correct number of staff and their skill level with the requirements of producing the menu items.

Effect on Service Staff

Service may be affected if the new menu item is served in special dishware, if it needs an extra piece of service ware, or if the production of the item impedes the flow of service. An item requiring extra preparation time might require retraining of service personnel, who must notify the kitchen early in order to keep a complete table's order together. Service personnel will also need to be trained to identify, describe, and answer customer questions about the new menu items for the new items to be effectively sold.

Activity

Profit and Competitive Position

Joey's Restaurant has been in business for five years. Joey has been moderately successful with entrées of mostly sautéed or deep-fried items. He also offers coleslaw, baked potatoes, and French fries to accompany these entrées. His cooking equipment consists of a range top with four gas burners, an oven, and a deep fryer.

Regular customers have begun asking for some new menu items because the menu has not changed since Joey opened the restaurant. He is considering some healthier menu items, such as broiled fish, fresh vegetables, and green salads. However, he is not sure he can prepare these items with the equipment he has. He also is not sure his cook has the skill or time to prepare them.

1 What equipment might Joey need that he does not now have to provide the new choices?

_____
_____
_____
_____
_____
_____
_____

2 What can he do to help the cook prepare the new menu items?

_____
_____
_____
_____
_____
_____
_____

3 Are there other things he should consider before changing his menu?

_____
_____
_____
_____
_____
_____

Summary

Planning a menu involves identifying and selecting menu items for inclusion in a restaurant's menu. Aspects to consider include the target market, the sales potential of the proposed menu items, other restaurants that will compete for the same customers, current restaurant industry trends, and consumer trends. When developing a restaurant menu, it is important to understand the marketing environment in which it exists, including an assessment of competitors' menu offerings and pricing parameters. Consumer trends include a demand for healthier menu offerings, Asian fare, and quick, family meals offered at a reasonable price. In addition, the restaurant industry is very competitive, and one of the tools to success is to create a strong brand image in the minds of target customers. A well-planned menu and its superb operational execution help to reinforce the restaurant's brand image, leading to financial success.

The decision to include or exclude a menu item may depend upon more than customer tastes and preferences. It may also depend upon whether or not the item can be priced to meet the targeted profit margin and price point category the restaurant uses. Successfully executing a menu also must take into account operating efficiency and staff capability.

Review Your Learning

1 To begin the process of identifying menu items, it is useful to list

A. all the appetizer items first since they are first on the menu.

B. the categories of food items that will appear on the menu.

C. all the items that appear on your competition's menu.

D. all your favorite food items, whether they are good or not.

2 Which of these is a brand image *not* designed to do?

A. Create an image in consumers' minds

B. Generate customer loyalty and community visibility

C. Enable a high profit and return on investment

D. Define the goods and services offered

3 Your target customers are a group of people

A. who your investors have selected.

B. who spend a lot on eating out.

C. who presently come to your restaurant.

D. with similar demands in your market area.

4 Which of these is *not* considered a consumer trend?

A. Demand for low carbohydrate food items

B. Demand for healthier menu items

C. Interest in Asian cuisine

D. Demand for family meals at a good price

5 Target profit margins are

A. designed to make the restaurant the most money possible during the first year of operation.

B. designed to provide the owners and investors with a specific return on their investment.

C. not to be considered when pricing menu items because they have no impact.

D. not an important part of planning for a restaurant's success.

6 When considering the operating capability of a restaurant,

A. the skill level of the cooks is the most important factor to consider.

B. the number of cooks is the most important factor to consider.

C. the skill level of the servers and cooks is the most important factor to consider.

D. the number and skill level of cooks and servers are equally important.

7 It is a good idea when pricing menu items to price

A. everything to match prices of your direct competition.

B. everything high to increase profits.

C. everything at double the food cost.

D. items using price points similar to your direct competition.

8 When evaluating the sales potential of new menu items,

A. the items should be tested by the cooks, servers, and customers.

B. the items should be put on the menu and sold to see how well they do.

C. the most important consideration is whether they are available in competing restaurants.

D. contribution to profit should not be considered.

Meeting Nutritional Needs and Food Preferences of Customers

2

Inside This Chapter

- Factors Influencing Food Item Selection
- Sources of Nutritional Components on the Menu
- Nutritional Information for Customers
- Nutritional Cooking Methods
- Types of Vegetarian Diets
- Dealing with Customers Who Have Allergies

After completing this chapter, you should be able to:

- Outline the factors that influence food item selection by customers.
- Identify the sources of carbohydrates, proteins, and fats on the menu.
- Provide nutritional information to customers.
- Identify preparation and cooking methods that preserve nutrients in quantity cooking.
- Recognize the various types of vegetarian diets.
- Identify procedures for preparing food items for customers with allergies.

Test Your Knowledge

1. **True or False:** Customers select menu items based on their hunger alone. *(See p. 19.)*

2. **True or False:** The main sources of carbohydrates are fruit and vegetables. *(See p. 21.)*

3. **True or False:** A lacto-vegetarian would be comfortable selecting eggs from your breakfast menu. *(See p. 30.)*

4. **True or False:** It is important for servers to have a full understanding of all menu items to answer customer questions. *(See p. 32.)*

5. **True or False:** New England Clam Chowder would be acceptable to suggest to a customer with an allergy to dairy products. *(See p. 32.)*

Key Terms

Allergen

Calorie

Carbohydrate

Cholesterol

Complete protein

Fat

Hydrogenation

Incomplete protein

Lacto-ovo-vegetarian

Lacto-vegetarian

Lipid

Meat substitutes

Minerals

Nutrition

Organic food

Perishability

Polyunsaturated

Price-value relationship

Protein

Recommended Dietary Allowance (RDA)

Satiety value

Saturated fat

Trans fat

Unsaturated fat

Vegan

Vegetarian

Vitamins

Introduction

Customers select menu items for a variety of reasons. Planning an effective menu requires you to consider all these reasons in order to meet the diverse needs of customers. Since nutrition is an important customer concern, it also is necessary for you to understand the sources of carbohydrates, fats, and proteins in food items in order to plan a well-balanced menu. You also must know and follow the federal guidelines about the nutritional information that must be provided to customers.

The number of customers with special dietary needs has steadily increased in recent years. How your operation meets these needs could very well help you remain competitive. These special needs range from a variety of distinct vegetarian diets, religion-influenced diets, to diets for people allergic to various kinds of food items or ingredients. Procedures for providing information to customers are discussed in this chapter, as well as the techniques used to maintain the nutritional quality of food items through foodhandling and preparation.

Exhibit 2a

Customers consider a variety of factors before choosing a menu item.

Factors Influencing Food Selection

Why is a customer willing to pay $8.95 for a hamburger served on a plate in one restaurant, when in another restaurant the same hamburger is sold wrapped in paper for $2.99? When customers look at a menu, they are driven by many considerations in choosing the item they will order. (See *Exhibit 2a.*) These considerations include:

- Hunger
- **Nutrition** (the science of food, nutrients, and their actions in the body)
- Medical condition
- Merchandising
- Price
- Convenience
- Value
- Price-value relationship

Hunger is sometimes the main reason for selecting menu items or choosing to eat at all, but it is usually not the only force behind customers' decisions. Customers today are concerned with nutrition and the nutritional components of food items, whether they are consciously selecting an item based on its levels of carbohydrates, proteins, fats, or by some other factor that defines their particular dietary need.

Customers may have particular dietary needs because of a medical condition that requires them to be careful in menu item selection. However, customers are just as likely to order an item that is contrary to good nutritional advice because they are celebrating a special occasion or because they are rewarding themselves in some way. Menu planners have to take into account both these types of customers—those who are following a special diet of some kind and those who want to indulge.

Another factor that influences menu item selection is the merchandising done through television, print media, and other forms of advertising. Brand recognition is challenging and even difficult to establish, but once it has taken hold it can be particularly influential for customers making routine purchase decisions. Customers in your establishment can also be influenced by carefully designed menus, table tent cards, server suggestions, or other types of point-of-sale merchandising. Care must be taken to ensure that

Think About It...

What other factors can influence menu item selection?

the merchandising accurately represents what is actually served; otherwise, customers will feel misled and disappointed. In some states, misrepresenting menu items is against the law.

Price is an important selection tool for customers when selecting the restaurant or type of restaurant in which to dine. The price of the individual menu items can be an important factor, but a carefully designed menu can reduce the use of price as a selection tool. However, customers do want value for the price they pay. The customer, not the operator, defines the price-value relationship, which can be described as the customers' estimate of whether or not a received product or service meets their expectations.

Convenience is another important selection tool. It applies both to the convenience of the restaurant's location and the convenience of obtaining food items at the restaurant. Inside the restaurant, customers measure convenience by the promptness of service of food items, ease of consumption, and cleanup. Many restaurants have added take-out menus, delivery, drive-up windows, or curbside service to meet customers' needs for convenience. Once again, it is the customer that assigns the convenience value.

Activity

Why People Buy

Conduct a survey of at least five to ten class members or friends to determine why they select the restaurants and food items they do. When interviewing, ask open-ended questions that let people provide their own answers; do not ask questions with simple answers such as yes/no or agree/disagree.

1. Ask them to name three restaurants they visit often.

2. For each restaurant, ask for several reasons behind their choice of that restaurant.

3. For each restaurant, ask what three items they order most often.

4. Ask why they order those items.

5. Prepare a report of your findings.

6. In the report, include two tables.

   ☐ One table of the responses to Step 2 about why they chose the restaurants.

   ☐ One table of the responses to Step 4 about why they chose the items.

Think About It...

A calorie is an incredibly small amount of energy. Calories are the standard measure used in laboratory work about food. These energy units are so small that the calories referenced in the foodservice and food-packaging industries are actually kilocalories, equaling one thousand laboratory calorie units. For the sake of simplicity, the term "calorie" has become the accepted substitute in common usage outside the lab.

Sources of Nutritional Components on the Menu

The human body requires nutrition from three major food groups to provide **calories**—the amount of energy that a food contains—and other nutrients. Additionally, two other nutritional components have been identified as important by the United States Department of Agriculture (USDA), resulting in five items to take into account when planning menus:

- Major food groups
    - ☐ Carbohydrates
    - ☐ Fats
    - ☐ Proteins
- Other nutritional components
    - ☐ Vitamins and minerals
    - ☐ Water

Carbohydrates

Carbohydrates are important for the energy they provide as the digestive system breaks them down into glucose. Energy is measured in calories, and most carbohydrates provide approximately four calories for each gram consumed.

Exhibit 2b

Sources of carbohydrates include potatoes, vegetables, bread, pasta, and sugar.

The carbohydrate group consists primarily of sugars and starches. Sugars are simple carbohydrates, while starch are complex carbohydrates. The food items that contain carbohydrates include (see *Exhibit 2b*):

- White and sweet potatoes
- Fruit and vegetables
- Sugars and other sweeteners
- Grain-based food items such as bread, rice, cereal, and pasta

The USDA recommends that a healthy diet include two cups of fruit and two and one-half cups of vegetables per day for a person eating about two thousand calories. The fruit and vegetables consumed every day should include a variety selected from dark green vegetables, orange vegetables, legumes, starchy vegetables, and other vegetables. A minimum of three or more servings of whole grain is recommended for everyday consumption, while other grains products may be selected from enriched or whole-grain products. The consumption of sugars and other sweeteners should be limited.

Proteins

Proteins are required by the human body to promote growth, repair body tissue, and help regulate body functions. Proteins also provide energy at the rate of about four calories per gram.

Exhibit 2c

Source of proteins include meat, eggs, fish, milk, and beans.

Proteins are composed of approximately twenty different amino acids in varying amounts and combinations. Proteins are found in high amounts in these types of food (see Exhibit 2c):

- Meat
- Fish
- Poultry
- Eggs
- Dairy products

Proteins found in these animal products are considered complete proteins because they contain the nine essential amino acids required by the human body.

Proteins are also found in legumes, tofu and other soy products, cereals, seeds, and nuts. The proteins found in these kinds of food are considered incomplete proteins because they do not include all of the essential amino acids. However, they can be combined to provide all the essential amino acids needed throughout the day in a healthy diet.

To meet recommendations for consumption of proteins, a person eating about two thousand calories a day can consume approximately five ounces of lean meat, fish, or poultry, plus three cups of fat-free or low-fat milk or equivalent milk products per day.

Exhibit 2d

Sources of fat include potato chips, chocolate, nuts, oil, and butter.

Fats

Fats are found in many kinds of food, but some food items have a much higher percentage of fat than others. Examples include (see *Exhibit 2d*):

- Butter
- Oil
- Nuts
- Potato chips
- French fries
- Pie crust
- Chocolate

Although they contribute to weight gain, **fats** are an important part of the human diet because they are needed to:

- Provide heat and energy
- Carry fat-soluble vitamins
- Promote essential body functions
- Act as protective padding around internal organs and the body as a whole

Fats provide approximately nine calories per gram and are considered high in **satiety value**—satisfaction value—because they break down slowly in the body. Fats are composed of long chains of carbon atoms that have many hydrogen atoms and very few oxygen atoms attached.

Fats, can be separated into saturated fats and unsaturated fats. **Saturated fats** have all the chains' available carbon bonds filled with hydrogen atoms. This type of fat is generally found in animal fats; however, cocoa butter and coconut oil also are quite saturated. **Unsaturated fats** are made up of carbon chains that have one or more spaces on the chain that do not hold a hydrogen atom. Unsaturated fats that are missing hydrogen in two or more places are described as **polyunsaturated.** Chemically, they are also described as having two or more unsaturated double bonds. This type of fat is generally found in fish oils and vegetable oils such as cottonseed, soybean, and corn. Unsaturated fats can undergo a process called **hydrogenation** in which hydrogen is added to the chain, thereby making the unsaturated fat into a saturated fat.

If a fat remains slightly unsaturated after processing, the fat can change shape. These fats are known as trans fats. Nutrition experts recommend that trans fats be consumed in very small amounts.

According to the USDA, fats should make up less than 30 percent of a human diet, and saturated fats should make up less than 10 percent of the calories consumed in the diet.

Cholesterol

Cholesterol is a lipid, a type of molecule related to the fat family. Cholesterol is found in animal products such as beef fat, eggs, and dairy products. Consuming large amounts of cholesterol is a risk factor for heart attack and stroke in some people. For a healthy diet, experts recommend consuming less than three hundred milligrams of cholesterol daily.

When planning a menu, consideration should be given to reducing the number of menu items offered that are high in fat, particularly saturated fat and trans fats, and those containing cholesterol.

Vitamins and Minerals

Varying amounts of vitamins and minerals are found in all food items. Some kinds of food are higher in certain vitamins and minerals and are known as good sources of these nutrients. (See *Exhibit 2e.*) Vitamins and minerals are a necessary part of the human diet because they work individually or in combination to promote essential body processes.

- Vitamins may be water-soluble or fat-soluble. Water-soluble vitamins include vitamin C and the B-complex vitamins. Fat-soluble vitamins include vitamins A, D, E, and K.

- Minerals may be required in relatively large amounts, such as calcium, sodium, and potassium, or in trace amounts, such as iron, zinc, and iodine.

The Recommended Dietary Allowance (RDA) for many vitamins and minerals has been established by the USDA. For example, the USDA recommends that consumption of the mineral sodium (salt) be limited to twenty-three hundred milligrams per day—the equivalent of a teaspoon. The RDAs are reviewed, added to, and changed every five years.

The USDA also recommends that these essential nutrients be consumed through food items rather than by taking pills. Unfortunately, the quality and usefulness of vitamins and minerals can be changed by the way food items are prepared (which is explained later in this chapter). Nevertheless, providing a variety of food items on a menu—and preparing them properly—can help customers consume the necessary vitamins and minerals. The menu might then offer:

Exhibit 2e

Some kinds of food are higher in certain vitamins and minerals.

- Lean meats, poultry, and fish that are grilled or broiled rather than deep-fried

- Fresh salads served with dressing on the side

- Fresh fruit desserts

- Vegetables that have been steamed

- Baked potatoes as an alternative to French fries

- Whole-grain breads or rolls instead of only white bread

- Vegetarian entrées

These are but a few ways to meet the needs of customers with nutritional concerns.

Water

Water is a necessary component of the human diet. Water takes part in chemical reactions, is the major ingredient in bodily fluids, acts as a lubricant, aids in the regulation of body temperature, and removes waste from the body. Humans engaged in heavy physical activity might require more water to maintain necessary levels of fluid in the system because water is lost through sweat.

Water is found in larger amounts in beverages, soups, fruit, and vegetables and in smaller amounts in other kinds of food. Nutritionists recommend that humans consume six to eight glasses of fluid per day—in addition to the water in food items—to maintain optimal bodily functions.

Activity

Food Group Quiz

Assign the following menu items to the food group with which they are most closely associated. Write the letter of the food group in the space in front of the menu item. Food groups may be used as many times as needed.

Food Groups	Menu Items
A. Simple carbohydrates	____ **1** Kidney beans
B. Complex carbohydrates	____ **2** Maple syrup
C. Proteins	____ **3** Roast beef
D. Saturated fats	____ **4** Rye bread
E. Unsaturated fats	____ **5** Basil vinaigrette
	____ **6** Raspberry sauce
	____ **7** Hydrogenated vegetable oil
	____ **8** Whole wheat rolls
	____ **9** Mayonnaise
	____ **10** Italian dressing

Nutritional Information for Customers

The Food and Drug Administration (FDA) is the federal agency responsible for defining labeling laws for food items. The current requirements for labeling apply to packaged consumer food items sold in grocery stores. The labels provide information to the consumer on calories, calories from fat, total fat in grams, saturated fat, cholesterol, sodium, total carbohydrate, dietary fiber, sugars, protein, vitamins A and C, iron, and calcium. The labels indicate the percentage of each of the nutrients found in a defined portion size based on a two thousand calorie-per-day diet.

Exhibit 2f

Hot and Sour Shrimp Soup
A classic Szechuan Chinese soup reputed to be good for colds. It contains vinegar for the sour and chili oil and white pepper for the hot. Two servings. *(395 calories, 36 grams carbs, 30 grams protein, 13 grams fat)* **$8.95**

Grilled Swordfish
Our manager's favorite! A charcoal-grilled swordfish served with asparagus, Portobello mushrooms, fresh chopped tomatoes, and brown rice. *(340 calories, 36 grams carbs, 37 grams protein, 6 grams fat)* **$13.95**

Seafood Lasagna
Try this spin on traditional lasagna. Instead of ground beef, our seafood lasagna contains shrimp, calimari, mussels, and salmon. Instead of a tomato sauce, ours has a white wine and parmesan cheese sauce. And finally, instead of traditional lasagna noodles, ours has whole wheat noodles and vegetables. *(418 calories, 51.8 grams carbs, 34.4 grams protein, 9.9 grams fat)* **$14.95**

Some restaurants choose to include nutritional information on their menu.

Nutritional Information in Restaurants

Some restaurant operations have chosen to offer nutritional information to their customers by using handouts, table tent cards, Web sites, or other merchandising tools. Some place it directly on the menu. (See *Exhibit 2f.*) However, such labeling of items listed on a restaurant menu is not required unless the menu indicates a nutritional or health claim for a particular menu item such as "heart healthy" or "low fat." The requirement for a claim of low fat, for example, is that the food item contains three grams of fat per serving or less.

Organic Food in Restaurants

Another trend towards healthier eating includes the interest in and use of organic food. **Organic food** is defined by the USDA as those food items grown by farmers that emphasize the use of renewable resources and the conservation of soil and water to enhance environmental quality for future generations. Organic meat, poultry, eggs, and dairy products come from animals that are given no antibiotics or growth hormones. Organic food is produced without using most conventional pesticides, petroleum-based fertilizers or sewage sludge-based fertilizers, bioengineering, or ionizing radiation. Before a product can be labeled "organic," a government-approved certifier inspects the farm where the food item is grown to make sure the farmer is following all the rules necessary to meet USDA organic standards. Food that is labeled "organic" according to the USDA requirements may be advertised as such on the menu.

Some challenges presented by the use of organic food items include their higher cost and their **perishability**—the likelihood of spoilage or decay—due to a lack of preservatives. These two factors can increase the cost of menu items prepared from organic food items, which may necessarily lead to an increase in menu prices for such items.

27

Nutritional Cooking Methods

Nutritional cooking methods should be employed in all foodservice operations to maximize the nutrition available from the food items served. Nutritional cooking methods are not limited just to the cooking itself; they also include steps prior to cooking that preserve nutritional value, such as:

■ Type of processing

■ Handling at the foodservice operation

■ Preparation

Type of Processing

Maintaining a food item's nutrient content starts at the initial point of processing. Food items such as vegetables that are freshly picked and quickly frozen retain more nutrient content than a similar food item that is canned or not processed promptly. To maximize nutritional value, foodservice operations should purchase as much fresh and frozen food as possible, given profit margin profits.

Exhibit 2g

Freshly picked fruit and vegetables

Handling at the Foodservice Operation

As food items enter the foodservice operation, proper handling is important to maintain their nutrient content, as well as to maintain food safety standards. The person responsible for receiving food items should inspect them for quality and food safety upon arrival. If fresh fruit and vegetables have bruises or damaged skin, nutritional quality may already be reduced. Refrigerated and frozen food items should be checked for temperature. If the items have begun to thaw or have not been maintained at the proper refrigeration temperature, then some moisture loss will have already occurred and the water-soluble vitamins may be reduced. Meat, for example, loses B vitamins in the thawing process as the juices leave the meat.

Once food items have been received, they require prompt and appropriate storage. Most fresh fruit and vegetables are stored under refrigeration. (See *Exhibit 2g.*) They should not be kept tightly adjacent to another case of fruit or vegetables so they can continue to breathe. Frozen products of all kinds should be promptly stored in the freezer. Dairy products and other fresh food items such as meats, poultry, fish, and eggs are also stored using refrigeration. All products should be handled carefully to maintain food safety, quality, and nutrient content.

Food Preparation and Cooking

To maintain the nutrient content of food items served in the restaurant, the items should be received carefully, kept under proper storage, prepared as close to service time as possible, produced at the quantity most likely to be used quickly, and cooked as quickly as possible. The production processes of preparation and cooking should be evaluated to make sure that this happens.

Exhibit 2h

Cut fresh vegetables right before use. Do not cut them a day ahead of time and store them in water.

Vegetables

Vegetables are especially sensitive to poor preparation techniques. For example, potatoes should not be peeled and cut a day ahead of use and then stored in water because the ascorbic acid (vitamin C) may leach out. Other fresh fruit and vegetables also will maintain their nutrient components better if they are peeled and cut right before they are needed. (See *Exhibit 2h.*) To maintain the most nutrients in vegetables while they are being cooked, the vegetables should be steamed, prepared in small batches as needed, and not held longer than twenty minutes on a steam table.

Proteins, Carbohydrates, and Fats

Proteins, carbohydrates, and fats are more stable. However, if meats are cooked too far ahead of serving, they will continue to lose moisture and B vitamins. If the juices are preserved to make gravy or a sauce, some of the nutrient value can be retained. Fats that have been subjected to improper handling, such as being kept too hot or exposed to oxygen or light, may break down or oxidize. This chemical reaction results in an off-flavor and odor.

Activity

Fixing the Menu

You plan the menu for your restaurant, which is busy and profitable. However, you have received several comment cards in the last month from regulars asking you to offer a few healthier menu items. You have decided to look at two menu offerings to determine how they might be changed to meet your customers' needs.

Describe three changes you could make to each menu offering to make it healthier.

1 **Southern Fried Chicken:** One half chicken, deep-fried and served with whipped potatoes, creamy gravy, and Southern-style green beans with bacon and onions

_____

_____

_____

_____

2 **Lasagna:** Made with Italian sausage, four kinds of cheese, and egg noodles, and served with freshly baked white bread and Caesar salad

_____

_____

_____

_____

Types of Vegetarian Diets

Approximately 2.5 percent, or 4.8 million, of the adults in the United States follow a vegetarian diet of some kind on a consistent bases. Another 20 percent of the U.S. population indicates they usually maintain a vegetarian diet. Consumers choose to eat vegetarian diets for many reasons, including religious belief, concern for the environment, economics, health considerations, animal welfare factors, and ethical considerations related to world hunger issues.

A **vegetarian** is a person who consumes no meat, fish, or poultry products. There are different types of vegetarians (see *Exhibit 2i*):

■ A **vegan** follows the strictest diet of all and will consume no dairy, eggs, meat, poultry, fish, or anything containing an animal product or by-product. They consume only grains, legumes, vegetables, fruit, nuts, and seeds. They often even avoid using any product that contains animal components, such as leather shoes.

■ A **lacto-vegetarian** consumes all the above vegetarian items plus dairy products.

■ A lacto-ovo-vegetarian consumes all the above vegetarian items plus dairy products and eggs.

The National Restaurant Association reports that 80 percent of table-service restaurants offer vegetarian entrées to meet the needs of vegetarian consumers. Also, since many college students classify themselves as vegetarians, they are demanding such offerings from restaurant and dormitory foodservices at colleges. Another way that the needs of vegetarian consumers are being met is through the production of meat substitutes, including vegetable- and soy-based burgers, nondairy milk such as soy milk, and convenience vegetarian entrées. These products are also available to foodservice menu planners.

Exhibit 2i

Types of Vegetarian Diets

✓ = does eat or use ✗ = does not eat or use	Grains	Legumes	Vegetables	Fruit	Nuts	Seeds	Eggs	Dairy	Meat	Fish	Poultry	Animal By-Products
Vegan	✓	✓	✓	✓	✓	✓	✗	✗	✗	✗	✗	✗
Lacto-vegetarian	✓	✓	✓	✓	✓	✓	✗	✓	✗	✗	✗	✓
Lacto-ovo-vegetarian	✓	✓	✓	✓	✓	✓	✓	✓	✗	✗	✗	✓

Addressing Food Allergies

Preparing food items for customers with allergies can be a challenge, since many of the most common food allergens—substances that produce an allergic reaction—are found in restaurant kitchens on a daily basis. (See *Exhibit 2j* on the next page.) These common allergens include:

■ Peanuts and tree nuts

■ Wheat

■ Soy and soy products

■ Milk and dairy products

■ Eggs and egg products

■ Fish and shellfish

Exhibit 2j

Some types of food with allergens

Foodhandling and Preparation for Food Allergies

The types of food that are likely allergens should be kept separate from other food items in the kitchen. In the case of fish and dairy products, they should be separated as a usual practice to prevent cross-contamination. A safe kitchen will have all food-item components properly identified and stored separately from each other.

When preparing food items for a customer with a known allergy, all the utensils, cookware, service ware, and equipment used must be cleaned, sanitized, and allergen-free. All care should be taken to prevent the menu item from coming into contact with the allergen.

Assisting Customers with Food Allergies

Most customers with a food allergy will volunteer this information. They are generally able to be quite specific about the kinds of food to which they are allergic. The server should heed these restrictions and take one of two actions, depending on what is possible:

- **Suggest alternative menu item choices.**

- **Make adjustments to the food item's recipe.** This action is most easily done when a garnish or other item can simply be omitted from the recipe (e.g., omitting nuts on a salad). When this is the solution, the server must instruct the cooking staff about the change.

Both of the above actions depend on the knowledge of the staff about allergens in the food items that they prepare and serve. Servers and cooks should know all the ingredients of each menu item. This will help the server answer customers' questions about menu items, and it may help prevent a cook from adding something to a menu item that would harm the customer.

One way to help prevent a mistake in production or service is to routinely serve sauces, salad dressings, and other garnishes separately from the menu item with which they are usually served. This gives the customer the choice in using or avoiding the product. This procedure in production and service is also useful for the vegetarian menu items discussed in the previous section.

Summary

It is important to recognize that customers select menu items for a variety of reasons, including hunger, nutrition, indulgence, dietary restriction, price, value, convenience, and merchandising. Customers also have expectations of menu choices that will help them meet their nutritional needs for carbohydrates, fats, and proteins. Receiving, storing, handling, preparing, cooking, and serving food items appropriately will help maintain their nutritional quality.

Customers may have needs for special types of food because they are vegetarians, have allergies to certain food components, or have other dietary restrictions. The FDA has issued requirements for providing nutritional information to consumers on packaged food items and for any dietary or health claims made on a menu.

Activity

Putting It All Together

You work at an upscale restaurant that prides itself on a well-balanced, nutritionally sound, but limited, menu. Customers expect to find interesting and high-quality items on the menu. They also are concerned about excess fat and carbohydrates; they tend to eat items that are more natural, and that have been prepared with nutrition-saving methods. Some regular customers are vegetarians, and some have allergies, but your restaurant prides itself on meeting their needs, too.

You plan the menu for this week. You have consulted with the chef and found that the following dishes are available for the menu. Your task is to select only five dinner entrées from the available choices so that the menu meets the needs of the expected customers. Defend your choices in the space provided on the next page.

Possible Dinner Entrées

■ **Apple-stuffed pork tenderloin with cinnamon raisin sauce**—472 calories, 6g fiber, 260mg sodium, 24g fat (11g saturated fat), 143mg cholesterol, 24g protein, 19g carbohydrate

■ **Beef medallions with pear-cranberry chutney**—250 calories, 3g fiber, 60mg sodium, 8g fat (3g saturated fat), 65mg cholesterol, 25g protein, 23g carbohydrate

■ **Beef Stroganoff**—599 calories, 4g fiber, 275mg sodium, 34g fat (19g saturated fat), 112mg cholesterol, 26g protein, 42g carbohydrate

■ **Beef tenderloin in a mushroom-wine sauce**—225 calories, 1g fiber, 270mg sodium, 11g fat (5g saturated fat), 70mg cholesterol, 25g protein, 8g carbohydrate

■ **Chicken Paprikash**—619 calories, 5g fiber, 330mg sodium, 41g fat (25g saturated fat), 187mg cholesterol, 22g protein, 36g carbohydrate

■ **Deep-dish turkey pot pie**—671 calories, 4g fiber, 320mg sodium, 32g fat (15g saturated fat), 95mg cholesterol, 28g protein, 34g carbohydrate

■ **Fettuccini Alfredo**—644 calories, 4g fiber, 225mg sodium, 44g fat (28g saturated fat), 139mg cholesterol, 4g protein, 44g carbohydrate

■ **Strip steak with mango-peach salsa**—255 calories, 1g fiber, 260mg sodium, 8g fat (3g saturated fat), 65mg cholesterol, 25g protein, 22g carbohydrate

■ **Tilapia over vegetables and rice**—230 calories, 3g fiber, 330mg sodium, 7g fat (1g saturated fat), 55mg cholesterol, 23g protein, 22g carbohydrate

■ **Trout with orange and almond**—320 calories, 3g fiber, 550mg sodium, 18g fat (6g saturated fat), 75mg cholesterol, 24g protein, 19g carbohydrate

continued on next page

Putting It All Together *continued from previous page*

1 _____

_____

_____

_____

_____

_____

2 _____

_____

_____

_____

_____

_____

3 _____

_____

_____

_____

_____

_____

4 _____

_____

_____

_____

_____

5 _____

_____

_____

_____

_____

Review Your Learning

1 Fats can be separated into

   A. complex and simple.

   B. water-soluble and fat-soluble.

   C. saturated and unsaturated.

   D. allergies and allergens.

2 Food labeling laws are defined by the

   A. American Dietetic Association.

   B. Food and Drug Administration.

   C. National Restaurant Association.

   D. U.S. Department of Agriculture.

3 Protein food items include

   A. fish and legumes.

   B. apples and pears.

   C. celery and lettuce.

   D. beef and pickles.

4 Common allergens include

   A. peaches and pears.

   B. dairy food items.

   C. chicken and turkey.

   D. maple syrup.

5 To provide nutritional food items, it is important to

   A. peel potatoes a day ahead to be sure they are ready.

   B. deep-fry chicken to preserve nutrients.

   C. check in received products when you have time.

   D. store all products promptly in the appropriate storage.

6 Lacto-ovo-vegetarians will not eat

   A. grains.

   B. vegetables.

   C. fish.

   D. seeds and nuts.

7 To advise customers on food selection, servers need to know

   A. the major ingredients of each menu item.

   B. only the names of each menu item.

   C. only the prices of each menu item.

   D. all the ingredients of each menu item.

8 To meet the needs of many customers,

   A. sauces and dressings should be served on the side.

   B. sauces should be made from the chef's secret recipe.

   C. vegetarian vegetable soup can be made with beef broth.

   D. cooks should prepare food items exactly as written.

Notes

Menu Layout and Design

Ken Parmesan ....
eless, skinless chicken breast seasoned
th herbs, lightly breaded & pan-fried.
aked with herb marinara sauce

Chicken Breast Ala Marsala .... $13.!
Boneless breast of chicken delicately
seasoned with herbs, sauteed with fresh
mushrooms & sweet marsala wine

Center Cut Pork Chops ....
Broiled to perfection. Served with apple-
sauce and herb roasted potatoes

Francisco's Pepper Steak ....
Beef tenderloin medallions sauteed in
butter with fresh mushrooms, sweet
bell peppers & onions

ho Fried Shrimp ....
....d and deep-fried. Se

3

Inside This Chapter

- Purposes of the Menu

- Relationship of Menu Design to Marketing

- Menu Psychology

- Menu Layout and Design Principles

After completing this chapter, you should be able to:

- List and describe the purposes of a menu.

- Explain how the menu communicates and reinforces the foodservice operation's brand.

- Explain how the menu reinforces marketing.

- Explain how the menu is a powerful sales tool.

- Explain how the menu can guide customers to select desired items.

- Explain how to use menu layout and pricing psychology to influence customer purchases.

- Explain the principles of menu layout and design.

Test Your Knowledge

1. **True or False:** The menu is designed around the listed menu offerings and their prices. *(See p. 40.)*

2. **True or False:** Menus using special typefaces and a moderate amount of white space have a positive influence on the customer. *(See pp. 47–49.)*

3. **True or False:** A menu item's placement on the menu can affect a customer's selection. *(See p. 43.)*

4. **True or False:** A restaurant's décor theme should influence menu design. *(See p. 39.)*

5. **True or False:** The menu and its offerings should match the expectations of the target customer. *(See pp. 40–41.)*

Key Terms

Leading	Type size
Margin	Type weight
Market segmentation	Typeface
Merchandising	Value pricing
Points	White space

Introduction

The menu is the single most important sales and marketing tool available to a restaurant. It is an extremely valuable tool because it serves so many purposes. A well-designed menu communicates much more than just a list of your available food items. It declares and reinforces the restaurant's brand identity to your customers. It does full-time duty as a promotional information channel for the operation. It works hard as an internal communications tool, too, since it is a virtual guide to purchasing, planning, production, and service. Last, but not least, this multifaceted tool can literally be put directly into the hands of a restaurant's entire staff and customer base.

Done correctly, all these elements combine into an impressive, effective vehicle that ultimately does one thing extremely well: sell product and generate profit in a highly competitive business.

Exhibit 3a

Back-of-the house employees use the menu to plan and organize their work.

Purposes of the Menu

A menu serves many purposes. It is the most important sales and communication tool available to the restaurant operator. It communicates to customers what is available for purchase, and it encourages customers to purchase certain items according to their placement on the menu. It communicates to back-of-the-house staff what must be prepared (see *Exhibit 3a*), and it communicates to front-of-the-house staff what is available for sale and at what price. It also organizes the meal into courses and reinforces the brand identity of the operation.

External Uses

The menu lists the products and services offered for sale in the restaurant. In fact, in most restaurants, the menu includes the only items available for sale. As your primary communication with the customer, the menu should be very clear as to what products and services are offered and what is included in the price for each.

Brand Identity

The menu reinforces the brand identity of the operation through the menu items offered, the way they are presented, and the use of layout and design principles. All these things should be consistent with the brand identity.

- The type of dining that the operation targets should be consistent with the style of the menu, the size of the menu, whether or not there is a children's menu, whether or not there is a wine list, etc. For example, a fine-dining establishment should have a cultured and reserved-looking menu on fine paper; it should not have a plastic-laminated, circus-themed menu.

- The prices listed in the menu should be consistent with the price category of the operation. Customers should not be surprised by how high or how low the prices on the menu are, after the marketing and advertising teams have positioned the pricing. Also, the price position and style should fit with the price category.

- The style of the menu should be consistent with the décor of the restaurant. For example, if the restaurant specializes in Western cuisine, the menu and the typeface should have a Western look, the language should reflect a "Western" dialect, and there probably should be some Western graphics included.

- The color scheme of the menu should match the color scheme of the operation.

Think About It...

There are restaurants without menus. How do these establishments know what to buy, cook, serve, and sell?

- Logos used on the menu should be the same as those used elsewhere.

- Even the way in which the menu is presented to the customer should be consistent with the brand identity. For example, a quick-service restaurant should not have a cultured and reserved-looking menu on fine paper that is formally presented to the customer after being seated at the table; it should be posted on the wall.

Merchandising is the element of marketing that is concerned with the sale of goods and services to customers. It includes advertising, product display, pricing, discounts, special offers, the invention of sales pitches, and the identification of avenues for sales. The menu is the point-of-purchase merchandising tool used most by customers in a restaurant. Because of this, the menu is the restaurant's most effective, and possibly only, sales tool.

Internal uses

In an efficient foodservice operation, the menu is used internally. These uses include:

- Determining what equipment is needed to support the menu

- Defining what food items should be purchased and kept in inventory

- Helping develop a production schedule of what food items need to be prepared and when

- Determining the number and skill level of production and service personnel required to effectively execute the menu

Relationship of Menu Design to Marketing

A basic principle of marketing requires that you define your target market—the group of customers whose needs will be met by your product or service offerings. These target customers are selected from all possible customers based on some group of common characteristics. The rationale behind defining the target market is that it is very difficult to meet the needs of every possible customer. With that in mind, most menus are developed to attract and meet the needs of your target market. (See *Exhibit 3b.*)

Exhibit 3b

A menu is developed
for your target market.

Target Market

Menu offerings should be created to appeal to your target customer. The décor of the operation must be planned with this customer in mind. The type of service provided should meet their needs. The price of the menu items should fit their income category. In total, the menu and its design should reinforce the relationship of the foodservice operation with the selected target market.

The target market may be divided into segments; this is called market segmentation. Common market segmentation dimensions include:

- Age (e.g., children)

- Income

- Occupation

- Special interest (e.g., theater patrons)

- Time of day (e.g., breakfast)

- Other distinguishing features

Different menu offerings, menu looks, and prices can be created to appeal to a specific market segment.

The Menu as Advertising

The menu is the only piece of advertising that the customer is sure to read. It is the primary sales tool of the operation. It can be used to draw attention to those items that are in some way unique or different from the competition. The menu can reinforce your brand at the point of sale.

If a customer has been reached through some other form of advertising, the customer already has developed some expectations of the restaurant and menu before arrival. The restaurant and menu should support the marketing that has been done, thus meeting the customer's expectations. The menu is a powerful sales tool if the expectations of the customer are met.

There are many ways that the menu can be used to market the restaurant. Some of the most commonly used methods include:

- Making the menu available in its original or smaller form for customers to take when they leave the restaurant

- Providing copies for newcomers in the area

- Distributing copies to local businesses

- Giving copies to tourism organizations

Activity

Madison Avenue Battle for the Account

You work in a large Madison Avenue advertising firm that specializes in promoting restaurants. A possible new account is a large, but relatively unknown, restaurant chain. If your firm can develop the most ideas for using their menu to promote the restaurant, you will win the account. Can you think of additional ways to distribute the menu outside the restaurant? Compete against other ad agencies to see who wins the new account. Allow yourselves ten minutes to make your pitch.

Menu Psychology

The menu has been called the most effective sales and marketing tool available to the restaurant operator. Its purpose is to sell the items the operator wants to sell. Menu planners, however, must first define those items. There are many strategies to use in selecting the items to be emphasized or "favored" on the menu:

- Favor the items that require the least labor, thereby saving labor cost.

- Favor the unique or differentiated item—called a signature item—that can only be found in your restaurant.

- Favor the items that have the largest margin—difference between food cost and selling price—and, therefore, contribute the most money to profit.

A combination of all these strategies may be the most effective. Whatever the rationale, some thought should go into determining which of the menu items should be the ones that customers are influenced to buy—your favored menu items.

Menu Layout Psychology

Once the favored menu items have been determined, their layout on the menu must be intelligently determined to maximize the sale of these items.

Placement on the Page

Placement of items on the menu is very important. The favored items should be placed in the most noticeable locations—where customers' eyes naturally focus. This is important because a customer can be encouraged to buy the items that are listed in these locations.

- On a single-page menu, the customer's eye initially goes up from the center and then near the bottom of the page. The most favored position is the center or just above the center of the page (see the left-hand side of *Exhibit 3c),* and this is where to place your favored menu items on a single-page menu.

- On the most common single-fold menu or book-style menu, the eye starts at the upper right, goes to the upper left, then down the left-hand page, then back to the right-hand page below the upper right corner, then down the right-hand page, and then toward the center of the menu. The most favored position is near the upper right-hand corner of the page (see the right-hand side of *Exhibit 3c).* This is where to place your favored menu items on a single-fold menu or on each two-page spread of a book-style menu.

Exhibit 3c

Single-Page Focus Point | **Double-Page Focus Point**

Placement at the Beginning or End of a List

Another way to sell the items that are profitable is to list them first or last in a list of similar items. This is because the beginning and end of a list are more memorable than the middle of a list, with the beginning being slightly more memorable than the end. Therefore, the appetizer you want to sell should be listed first in the list of appetizer and the appetizer that is your second choice should be listed last. Likewise, the salad, entrée, or dessert you want to sell should be listed first or last in their respective lists, and the same would apply to specialty or alcoholic beverages.

Use of Graphics

Graphics—drawings and photos—can be used to draw attention to the item you want to sell. Reinforce your brand by using the logo next to those items you want to sell, or surround the favored items with a box or other similar attention-grabber that supports your brand.

Use of Different Type

A different color type can be used to highlight the items you want to sell. Bold type or unusual typefaces, if used carefully, can also draw attention to those profitable items.

Item Pricing Psychology

Another aspect of menu psychology is pricing. The prices on the menu often, but not always, affect what customers select. As such, it is an important aspect of selling your wares. Pricing is a function of competition, demand, and costs. The next chapter will discuss pricing theories in more detail, but there are some elements of pricing that should be considered here.

Exhibit 3d

Traditional Placement of Price

led Sausage
rilled homemade Italian sausage
ell peppers, onions & mushrooms, served with
nerb roasted potatoes $9.50

Chicken Florentine
Boneless breast of chicken topped with fresh
mushrooms and mozzarella cheese, served on
a bed of sauteed spinach $13.95

Chicken Parmesan
Boneless, skinless chicken breast seasoned with
herbs, lightly breaded & pan-fried. Baked with
herb marinara sauce $13.95

Chicken Breast Ala Marsala
Boneless breast of chicken delicately seasoned
with herbs, sauteed with fresh mushrooms &
sweet marsala wine $13.95

Center Cut Pork Chops
Broiled to perfection. Served with applesa
and herb roasted potatoes $13.95

Francisco's Pepper Steak
Beef tenderloin medallions sauteed in
with fresh mushrooms, sweet bell pe
onions $14.50

bo Fried Shrimp
and deep-fried. S

Improved Placement of Price

led Sausage
filled homemade Italian sausage
asted bell peppers, onions & mush-
rooms, served with herb roasted potatoes $13.95

Chicken Florentine ....
Boneless breast of chicken topped with
fresh mushrooms and mozzarella cheese,
served on a bed of sauteed spinach $13.95

Chicken Parmesan ....
Boneless, skinless chicken breast seasoned
with herbs, lightly breaded & pan-fried.
Baked with herb marinara sauce $13

Chicken Breast Ala Marsala ....
Boneless breast of chicken delicately
seasoned with herbs, sauteed with fresh
mushrooms & sweet marsala wine ....

Center Cut Pork Chops ....
Broiled to perfection. Served with apple-
sauce and herb roasted potatoes

Francisco's Pepper Steak ....
Beef tenderloin medallions sauteed in
butter with fresh mushrooms, sweet
bell peppers & onions

bo Fried Shrimp ....
and deep-fried. S

Placement of Prices

The placement of the prices on the menu affects purchase decisions. It is recommended that prices be listed directly at the end of the description of the item as shown on the right-hand side of *Exhibit 3d*, rather than before the item or next to the item name as shown on the left-hand side of *Exhibit 3d*. If price is the first thing a customer sees, then price becomes more important in the selection decision. Unfortunately, the use of dots from the end of the menu item name to the price listed on the right-hand side of the menu page invites customers to look at price.

Exhibit 3e

Quick-service market

Low-End Value Pricing

Value pricing—pricing your products and services based on their worth in usefulness or importance to the buyer—is prevalent in the quick-service market. (See *Exhibit 3e.*) Prices tend to be under $7.00 in this market, and the most common ending digit for the price is "9," as in $2.99. This is because people tend to round the price down to the nearest dollar (or at least dime). So a $2.99 price is mentally thought of either as "above $2.00" or as "about $2.90."

The quick-service market is a highly competitive market, and the price-to-value perception is very important. Because of rising costs of ingredients, utilities, and labor, prices may have to be raised. Customers perceive breaking the dollar barrier as a large increase. If a menu item that was previously considered "above $2.00" is repriced to "above $3.00," the higher perceived price may lead to a reduction in sales for that item.

If the price increase is necessary, it is better to increase the price substantially than to increase it slightly. For example, $2.99 should be raised to $3.29 rather than $3.09. In the eyes of the customer, both prices are "above $3.00," but the profit to the operation is increased if the higher price is used.

Another expectation of customers in the quick-service market is that there is not a wide variation in price between the most and least expensive items.

Exhibit 3f

Basic mid-range market

Mid-Range Value Pricing

Prices in the mid-range market tend to end in "5" more often than in "9," as in $7.95 instead of $7.99. (See *Exhibit 3f.*) Customers typically perceive both these prices as "above $7.00 and less than $8.00."

Again, the challenge becomes what to do if a price increase is necessary. If the items available on your menu are similar to items on competitors' menus, then the prices are market driven, and raising your prices ahead of the competition will reduce your sales. If the items available on your menu are unique or differentiated in some way from the competition, then an increase in prices is not as harmful to sales. The recommendation in the market-driven case is to hold off the price increase as long as possible, and then increase the price substantially when the barrier is broken. This strategy may help recoup lost profits experienced before the price was raised.

Exhibit 3g

Fine-dining market

Upscale Value Pricing

Prices for the upscale or fine-dining markets tend to end in 0, as in $17.00. Many operations have elected to leave off the dollar sign, the decimal point, and the zeros, and list the menu price as "17" at the end of the description of the product. This type of restaurant is also likely to offer a signature dish, one that is so unique or differentiated that there is no comparison price. In this style of restaurant, price is considered part of the dining experience. When thinking about price, the customer considers the service, the quality of food, and the ambience. (See *Exhibit 3g*.) The perception of value in this situation is very different from that in the quick-service market, although both kinds of customers have an expectation of value for the price.

Menu Layout and Design Principles

The menu is the tool used to communicate and sell the items offered in a restaurant. For it to be an effective communicator and sales tool, solid principles of layout should be applied. This section lists and explains those principles.

General Comments

In general, the following principles should be adhered to:

- When it is handed to the customer, the overall look of the menu should be appealing.

- The cover of the menu should reinforce the décor of the restaurant and be thematically consistent.

- Traditionally, a cover includes the logo or name of the restaurant. However, as it is the first opportunity to sell the menu items, some restaurants have added a short description of what the customer will find inside the menu, or a welcome or introduction to the restaurant.

- The cover (or typically the back cover) is also often used to provide such information as the address, telephone number for reservations, and name of the owner of the restaurant.

Readability

Once the customer opens the menu, it should be something that the customer can read. The use of good design principles will help in this regard.

Menus should have the following design characteristics:

- Written in plain language
- Printed in an easily readable typeface and size
- Uncluttered
- Organized to help customers find what they want

Exhibit 3h

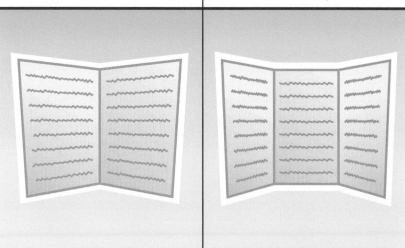

Single-fold menu   **Trifold menu**

Size and Shape

The size and shape of the menu are important considerations. The size should be such that the customer can handle the menu easily. Customers frequently sit down to read the menu and then discuss its contents with other members of their party. Doing this is difficult if the menu is too large. If the restaurant serves breakfast, lunch, and dinner, and the menu becomes too large, a separate menu for each meal will reduce the problem.

The most common menu shape is a single-fold menu—hinged in the center like a book. Menus also could be a single page or a trifold in which the right and left panels fold over or meet in the center. (See Exhibit 3h for both examples.) Some menus are displayed on menu boards on the wall and are not handed to the customer.

Internal Organization

Once the menu planners have determined what categories of food items to offer, headings should be used to indicate these categories on the menu. The headings should be in at least 18-point type. If you include a list of many entrées, it is more effective to separate the categories into subcategories: Seafood, Beef, and Pasta, for example.

Type Sizes and Faces

Type size—size of a letter or character—is measured in **points,** a unit of measurement; there are 72 points per inch. A 72-point letter would be 1″ high. The names of the items offered are best printed in at least 12-point type (⅙″), while descriptions should be no less than 10-point type. (See *Exhibit 3i.*) If the restaurant décor is such that it is quite dimly lit, the type sizes should be larger.

Exhibit 3i

**Examples of
Type Sizes**

10 point Helvetica

12 point Helvetica

18 point
Helvetica

24 point
Helvetica

Exhibit 3j

Examples of Typefaces

Serif Typefaces

Bookman

Didot

Garamond

Palatino

Times Roman

Sans Serif Typefaces

Century Gothic

Franklin Gothic

Gill Sans

Helvetica Neue

Specialty Typefaces

Brush Script

Copperplate

Linotext Old English

Shelly Allegro

Zapfino

Exhibit 3k

Examples of Type Weights

Lightweight type

Medium-weight type

Bold-weight type

Ultra-bold (heavy) weight type

You should also have available a large-print version of the menu for visual impaired guests.

Additionally, the use of uppercase and lowercase letters adds to readability. Menu category headings can be done in all uppercase letters, as can the item names. If the item names are in a foreign language, do not use all uppercase letters for the item names because they may be difficult to interpret. The use of uppercase and lowercase letters in descriptions of the menu items also adds interest.

The selection of the typeface—the look and style of the letter—is also important. (See *Exhibit 3j.*) Typefaces are available in many styles. There are two major categories of typefaces:

- **Serif**—Letters have tiny cross marks at the ends, such as Times Roman, Bookman, Palatino, and Garamond.

- **Sans serif (without serifs)**—Letters have plain ends, such as Helvetica, Century Gothic, and Franklin Gothic.

Some menu designers choose italics, script, or other special typefaces because they support the theme or décor of the restaurant. Such scripts or typefaces could include:

- Cursive handwriting
- Casual handwriting
- Engraved invitations
- Foreign (e.g., German)
- Historical (e.g., Old English)
- Curlicues
- Animals

There are literally thousands of typefaces available. Special typefaces are more difficult to read, but they can be used to good effect if the menu is not too long or detailed. Keep in mind that clarity and readability must take precedence over creativity. The typefaces selected most often for menu use are Times Roman, Bookman, and Helvetica because they are easy to read and readily available.

Type Weight

The type weight—thickness of the characters (see *Exhibit 3k*)—also contributes to readability. Normal or medium-weight type is easiest to read on a menu, whereas lightweight type does not stand out well. Bold may be used for emphasis, but its overuse makes the menu look amateurish.

Color

The use of color on the menu can contribute to readability or hinder it. Strong contrast should exist between the background paper and the printed copy. Black ink on white or very light cream paper offers a good contrast and is easy to read. The use of other colors may support the brand identity, but they should be selected carefully.

White Space

Consideration must be given to the amount of space on a menu that is not used for menu copy. In fact, some experts indicate that approximately 50 percent of the menu should be blank space, also known as white space (even if the background is not white). An empty margin around the edge of the paper provides white space. The space between menu items and within the description of each menu item is important to readability. Leading is the term used to describe the vertical spacing between lines of type. Leading varies from 1 to 5 points in height. One-point leading would leave very little space between lines of type in the description, while 5-point leading would leave a larger amount of space between lines of type. Using 3-point leading is a good choice in most menu applications.

Terminology

The terminology used on a menu is important for several reasons. Good descriptions of menu items will help sell them. In the past, menu writers used exaggeration or superlative words to describe menu items, such as "mounds of roast beef" or "the biggest salad in town" to sell the menu items. This often led to disgruntled customers, when what they actually received did not meet their expectations.

This prompted the National Restaurant Association in 1984 to issue accuracy-in-menu guidelines designed to ensure that what was described on the menu matched what was actually served. The guidelines include these categories:

- Descriptions of quantity
- Accuracy in the use of quality indicators
- Use of brand names
- Product identification
- Points of origin

Descriptions should be truthful and accurate. If a particular brand of barbecue sauce is used in the preparation of an item, then indicate that on the menu with a trademark sign, but always use that barbecue sauce. If the menu indicates that butter is served on certain vegetables, then it would be inaccurate for the cook to put margarine on those vegetables. In other words, describing your menu items one way and serving them in another contradicts the accuracy-in-menu guidelines, whether the error occurs in purchasing or production.

Descriptions are best if they use food-related words. Methods of preparation, such as grilled or char-grilled, can be used, but the item must then actually be grilled over an open flame. A recipe description should include a list of most, if not all, main ingredients used in the preparation of a dish. Describing the flavor components in an imaginative way can sell an item, but you should also make clear to customers what is included in the preparation of the item. Be sure to list common allergens so people with allergies can avoid the item.

Long descriptions take up space and may confuse the customer. A good description is twenty-five words or less.

Activity

Menu Layout

You are the menu planner at Sally's Steaks. Among your many responsibilities is maintaining the menu layout of its single-fold menu. You have noticed that one of the menu items listed in the middle of your entrée list, Chopped Steak with Mushroom Sauce, is very good and that occasionally a customer mentions its high quality. You also know that it is easy to prepare and that each one sold contributes more profit than many other menu items. However, this item is not frequently selected by your guests.

List at least three things you could do on the menu layout to increase sales of this entrée.

1 _____

_____

_____

_____

2 _____

_____

_____

_____

3 _____

_____

_____

_____

Summary

The menu is the most important sales and marketing tool used in a restaurant. There are design and layout principles that help make the menu more effective as a sales tool. A good menu provides accurate information to the guest, is easy to read, is manageable in size and shape, and reinforces the brand identity of the restaurant. The menu is used for many purposes, some internal and some external. The menu provides a list of products and services offered to the customer and is an effective point-of-purchase merchandising tool. Internally, it is used for purchasing, production, and service. A good menu reinforces your relationship with your target market and serves as an advertising tool that your customer will read. It can be used externally if the menu is distributed to the public. A menu can be designed to influence customer purchase of the items you want to sell through the use of layout and pricing psychology.

Review Your Learning

1 **What is a target market?**

A. Group of customers you are trying to reach with your menu

B. Group of customers targeted by your competitors

C. Group of all possible customers in your market area

D. Group of people with common characteristics

2 **How can a menu be used internally?**

A. To be shared with the business and tourism organizations in town

B. To develop purchasing, production, and service tools

C. To advertise what you sell on television

D. To give to customers as they leave

3 **What kind and size of typefaces should be used on menus?**

A. Exotic and less than 8 points to reinforce the brand identity

B. Italics and less than 8 points on a very large menu

C. Plain and over 10 points in most applications

D. Bold and 10 points in most applications

4 **Color is important on the menu. What color combination is easiest to read?**

A. Iridescent green on orange

B. Creamy white on black

C. Black on very light cream

D. Navy blue on pink

5 **Which menu price is most likely to be used by a quick-service operation?**

A. $7.99   C. $9.95

B. $3.50   D. $3.99

6 **The price of a unique or differentiated item on your menu should be**

A. higher, because it is difficult for the customer to compare with other restaurants.

B. really low, so that when the customer sees how your restaurant compares with the competition, you will sell much more.

C. the same as your competitors, so that when the customer sees how your restaurant compares, your prices look fair and reasonable.

D. in bold print, so it is easy for customers to compare with other restaurants.

7 **Prices should be placed strategically to make them less a part of the decision-making process. The recommended placement of prices is**

A. at the end of a line of dots across from the name of the entrée.

B. on the left-hand side, before the entrée name.

C. dependent upon whether the operation is quick-service, mid-range, or upscale.

D. at the end of the description of the menu item.

8 **Which of these should your menu support?**

A. Customer expectations skewed by the competitor's atmosphere and price

B. Your operation's relationship with your target market

C. Expectations determined by marketing considerations and consumer psychology

D. Differentiated offerings that meet perceived value expectations

Menu Pricing

4

Inside This Chapter

- Use of Price in Strategic Marketing
- Impact of External Environment on Prices
- Pricing Strategies
- Pricing and Gross Profit Margin
- Pricing Methods
- Employee Meal Pricing

After completing this chapter, you should be able to:

- Explain the meaning of price and its use in strategic marketing.
- Describe the impact of the external environment on price.
- Outline a variety of pricing strategies used by an organization.
- List, compare, and contrast basic pricing methods.
- Explain methods for pricing employee meals.
- Explain the relationship of gross profit margin and profitability to pricing menu items.

Test Your Knowledge

■ **True or False:** The prices on your menu can help position your brand. *(See p. 54.)*

■ **True or False:** It is a good idea to match the competitors' prices for similar menu items to remain competitive and profitable. *(See p. 64.)*

■ **True or False:** Food cost percentage is basically the percentage of money spent on food in relation to sales. *(See p. 70.)*

■ **True or False:** A sales-oriented pricing objective emphasizes sales volume and is not concerned with profit. *(See p. 56.)*

■ **True or False:** World events and geography have nothing to do with menu pricing. *(See pp. 60–61.)*

Key Terms

Contribution margin	Marketing strategy	Profit and loss statement
Cost of food sold	Markup factor	Profit-oriented pricing
Disposable income	Mathematical price	Sales-oriented pricing
Food cost	Net loss	Set dollar amount markup
Food cost percentage	Net profit	Status quo pricing
Gross profit margin	Pricing objective	Straight markup
Income statement	Pricing strategy	Strategic marketing plan
Market segmentation	Product-bundle pricing	

Introduction

Price is an important part of a foodservice operation's strategic marketing plan. This chapter will discuss pricing objectives and the role of price in brand positioning. The external environment in which your restaurant operates often affects the prices you establish for your menu offerings, so you will learn about the effect of the external environment on pricing decisions. You will learn several pricing strategies and how they can be used to segment the market. Consumers also consider the prices of menu items when deciding what to order; however, they do not change their orders for a small price difference. Therefore you must understand consumer price sensitivity and how consumers evaluate price and economic value.

The prices a restaurant charges are part of its marketing strategy. So it is important to learn how price can be used to differentiate a competitive pricing strategy from a premium pricing strategy and how to segment the consumer market into customer groups. Finally, determining the actual price to set that will be competitive, cover all costs, and leave an adequate profit is best not left to guessing. There are many ways to arrive at a price. In this chapter you will learn four methods to calculate a price and two methods for determining employee meal prices.

Use of Price in Strategic Marketing

A **strategic marketing plan** is a description of markets and how a foodservice operation intends to approach them. It has several components designed to address the needs and wants of customers. A **marketing strategy** is the method selected by an organization to meet the needs of a defined group of customers through the products or services provided, the means of communication, the distribution channels, and last but not least, the price. This defined group of customers is called the target market or market segment— a subdivision of the total market based on common characteristics and similar factors of demand, resulting in a smaller group.

Price serves two roles in the marketing strategy: it determines profitability and it provides information to customers and potential customers. Price determines profitability by bringing in more dollars than the sum of all the costs for the product or service. Finally, price provides information to customers not only about the price of the menu item, but also about the market category in which the restaurant falls.

Pricing Objectives

An important component of the strategic marketing plan regarding price is setting the **pricing objective** or **pricing strategy**— how the price is to be determined. There are several types of pricing strategies:

- Profit-oriented pricing

- Sales-oriented pricing

- Status quo pricing

Profit-Oriented Pricing

Under the **profit-oriented pricing** strategy, prices are established to make a certain targeted level of profit. (See *Exhibit 4a* on the next page.) Sometimes the profit target is to achieve close to the foodservice operation's desired return on investment. Other times, the profit target is to achieve as high a profit as possible.

Exhibit 4a

Profit-oriented pricing targets a certain level of profit.

While setting the price to maximize profit would appear to be the best goal, it depends on good forecasts of costs and customer demands. This method works better in the short term because predicting these factors accurately is difficult. Setting prices to make a targeted level of profit is an easier long-term strategy.

Sales-Oriented Pricing

In the sales-oriented pricing strategy, the goal is to maximize sales volume, not profit. Sales-oriented pricing is used to increase sales and market share. In the short term, coupons offering discounts and sales of particular menu items may increase sales volume. In the long term, pricing is very competitive with similar restaurants.

The drawback to the sales-oriented pricing strategy is that, although it may lead to increased sales, building more volume may not lead to increased profits. This pricing strategy can work if *all* of the following are true:

- Services are very limited.

- There are no extra amenities provided.

- The product is easily produced.

- The costs of providing the product can be kept low.

Status Quo Pricing

The motivation behind the status quo pricing strategy is to maintain your competitive position relative to the other restaurants in your market. In this type of pricing, competitors try to match prices for similar offerings.

While remaining competitive is important, every operation has different costs associated with providing its products and services. With similar pricing structures, an operation with low costs could be profitable while an operation with higher costs might not be profitable. If status quo pricing is the selected strategy, close attention to costs, prices, and actual profits is necessary to keep costs low and still remain competitive.

Role in Brand Positioning

Price is used not only as a way to determine profitability, but also as an informational tool; price is used to position a brand (or restaurant) in the marketplace. There is quite a difference among different types of restaurants—e.g., quick service, family, and fine dining—in their décor, target markets, services, menu items, prices, and so on. (See *Exhibit 4b.*) These all have to fit together properly so the customer accepts the whole package.

Exhibit 4b

Types of Restaurants

Quick-service restaurant brand

Family restaurant brand

Premium restaurant brand

Price attracts some customers and repels others. Customers tend to base their perception of a product or service at least partly on price. Traditionally, higher prices result in less demand and sales, while lower prices increase demand and sales. However, research has shown that increasing prices, up to a point, increases sales because customers believe there is higher quality associated with a higher price. If customers' expectations are met at the higher price, they will pay it.

However, as mentioned in the previous chapter, the value received for the price paid is the *customer's perception*. The overall image of the product, including the menu layout and design, atmosphere, and type of service are all considered by the customer to be part of the price. These components can define a brand as a value brand, a prestige brand, or a brand somewhere in between. Therefore, selecting the market in which your restaurant will compete or deciding how to position your brand requires consideration of all these elements in order to establish price.

Impact of External Environment on Prices

The external environment in which a restaurant operates is important to its pricing strategies and profitability. The external environment includes:

- Competition
- Economic factors
- Costs associated with entering the market
- Geographic factors
- Other factors

Competition

The competition of a commercial foodservice operation includes several levels:

- **Direct competition** includes the restaurants that serve the same target market or group of customers. The tendency for setting prices with direct competition is to use competitive pricing. However, to be effective against this kind of competition, the restaurant must meet the needs and wants of the customer better than the competition. Because all restaurants in a geographical area offer the service of providing food away from home, they are considered competitors to some extent—some are more direct competitors than others (e.g., nearby ones, ones of the same type). To be competitive in this case, pricing has to strongly consider the value that the customer receives for the price.

■ **Corporate foodservice** is somewhat like a restaurant, but is not as easily researched. Some companies have an employee cafeteria and others have lunch catered in for employees. This results in keeping potential customers at their work site and away from your restaurant.

■ **Grocery stores,** as well as stand-alone convenience stores and those in gas stations, also compete for customers' food dollars in two ways. First, the customer has to believe that the benefits of eating in your restaurant are worth the extra cost to them, in comparison to buying food at the grocery store and preparing it at home. Second, some grocery stores provide ready-to-eat food that customers can buy instead of visiting your restaurant. Again, the customer has to believe that the benefits of eating in your restaurant are worth the extra cost.

■ **Diet and weight-loss services** provide competition in two ways. First, they change the eating habits of their customers, sometimes to the point at which they are no longer your potential customers. Second, some sell food to their customers, which keeps them from frequenting your restaurant.

Failure to consider all the levels of competition when preparing a pricing strategy can lead to unprofitability.

Economic Factors

The economic environment consists of factors that affect consumer purchasing power and spending patterns, such as income, cost of living, interest rates, savings patterns, and borrowing patterns. When establishing prices for a restaurant's offerings, consideration must be given to major economic trends in the local market as well as national trends. (See *Exhibit 4c* on p. 62.)

The distribution of income varies across consumers in the United States. This affects their interest in and ability to spend money in restaurants.

■ **Consumers with high incomes** are willing to spend money on luxury goods, including eating out. Their spending patterns are not significantly affected by current economic events and the pricing category for these customers can be high if they believe they are receiving a high-quality product.

■ **Consumers who are reasonably comfortable economically** usually still pay attention to their spending. They have some disposable income—the amount of income that can be used on discretionary spending after the household bills have been paid—and are an important market to most restaurateurs. Offering competitive prices may be a strategy for them.

■ **Consumers who have little extra money to spend** beyond their cost of living might be induced to purchase menu items priced in the value market—the low-price segment of the market.

Global Restaurants

For those restaurants that have entered the global market, the economies of other countries are important. These restaurants must study prices and trends to determine whether the consumer has money to spend on the restaurant's offerings. There are economic factors to consider as well. As the cost of products or the fuel to provide those products goes up, then pricing becomes more of a challenge in remaining profitable.

Other Economic Impacts

Other economic impacts on pricing include inflation, unemployment, and recession in the local market as well as on a national level. For example, the ability of consumers to spend money on restaurant fare is different in areas that are losing employment opportunities as compared to areas that are creating jobs. Adjustments must be made to remain profitable. For example, during a recession in a local market, an established restaurant could vary its menu to offer lower-priced entrées and still remain profitable.

Cost of Market Entry

Another economic consideration is the cost of entry into the market. Entering the restaurant industry requires a relatively small amount of capital in comparison to some industries, such as the hotel industry or heavy manufacturing. However, a restaurant does have an investment in a building, equipment, furnishings, and the like, whether these are purchased or leased. The location selected for the restaurant will also affect these costs. Pricing must take into consideration the costs associated with market entry and the property in order to provide a return or profit on the investment.

Exhibit 4c

Factors That Affect Pricing

Economy   Politics   Transportation

Geographic Factors

There are two important geographic shifts in the United States that may affect a restaurant. The population has grown in the South and the West, while it has tended to decline in the North and the East. Also, the population has left many urban areas to move to neighboring suburbs or more rural areas. At the same time, some segments of the population are moving back into cities, especially into "gentrified" areas. Some of the growing rural areas are developing smaller cities that provide services, restaurants, retail stores, and entertainment, but without the crime, congested traffic, and high property costs associated with larger metropolitan areas.

Another geographic impact is the location of the restaurant. Prices and costs are different in various parts of the country, and they do not always change proportionately. Also, if the restaurant is located in a tourist area, the prices may change throughout the year—the prices could be higher during the tourist season and lower in the off season.

Access to supplies is affected by geographic location as well. Fresh fish and seafood might be more available in a coastal location. However, other supplies may have to be delivered from a long distance, thereby increasing costs.

Other Factors

Other events outside of the control of the restaurant might affect costs, and consequently, pricing (See *Exhibit 4c*). These events include legislation at the local or national level, political issues, political action groups, trade limits with other countries, political

Weather   Time   Form

unrest that limits the ability of a country to supply their traditional products, etc. To remain competitive, restaurants need to be aware of current and future situations that impact costs in order to price menu offerings well.

Availability of products may also be influenced by political factors. The U.S. government could boycott products from a certain nation, or for safety reasons, could prohibit the import of a product. For example, the FDA recently banned the importation of green onions because of an outbreak of hepatitis A linked to a contaminated shipment of the vegetable.

Weather can also affect the cost of food. If severe storms, drought, or very cold temperatures hurt a specific geographical location's crops, the availability of a food supply could be limited. The associated cost for the product then increases, and a restaurant might have to consider altering its menu offerings or prices to account for these increased costs.

Finally, the form of the food item affects its cost. The more processing the raw food product undergoes, the more it costs. For example, grated cheese is more costly than blocks, and blocks of cheese are more costly than entire wheels. Also, more costly packaging needed to contain processed food results in added costs.

Pricing Strategies

Several factors must be taken into account when determining the pricing strategy for a foodservice operation. It is important to know what consumers in general are thinking about the products and prices in your market. It is even more important to know what *your* customers are thinking about *your* products and prices. Consumers are sensitive to prices, mostly in terms of getting good value for what they spend. You must set prices so your customers are satisfied. Usually, this involves a combination of psychological pricing and market segment pricing.

Consumer Price Sensitivity

Pricing strategies are dependent on an understanding of consumer behavior and the context of the pricing objectives. A restaurant can never know too much about its customers and the values they assign to a product or service.

Consumers are sensitive to price, especially to price increases. As noted in the previous chapter, consumers do not look at prices objectively, but relatively. A price range of $7.50 to $7.99, for example, is still in the upper $7.00 range. It is also considered to be much less than $8.00 in the consumer's perception.

Raising a price above the next dollar point, such as $8.00 in this example, requires careful consideration of the benefits and consequences. If customers are aware of price increases for particular items in grocery stores, or if they have heard in the media about a shortage or a damaged crop, they are more likely to accept a price increase. If a price increase is due to other costs of which customers are unaware, it can be more difficult for them to understand, and they will probably go elsewhere. Customers do have a perception of the prices of comparable items and expect these prices to remain competitive.

If a restaurant has positioned itself in a competitive pricing situation, price increases become more of a challenge. Restaurants tend to wait for another restaurant to raise prices before they do. This may mean that certain menu items will be unprofitable to the restaurant for a time. When a price is raised, as in the above example, it probably should be substantially more than $8.00. The customer perceives a price of $8.39, $8.50, or even $8.69 as a big increase, but all are in the $8.00 range and are much less than $9.00. So to recoup some of the profits lost when increased costs are not followed immediately by a increase in price, the new price should be in the middle of the $8.00 to $8.99 category.

Price and Economic Value

An alternative to price increases is price cutting. Offering price cuts is a way to increase sales volume. The price cuts can be offered through promotional discounts, coupons offering a free entrée when one of equal or higher price is purchased, and the like.

However, price cuts are not always received positively by consumers. They may think that a coupon offer indicates the restaurant is not doing well and needs to increase sales. Consumers may question the quality of the service or food, and may not want to take advantage of this offer.

Conversely, price increases may not always be perceived negatively. Customers may see a price increase as an improvement in quality, and therefore worth paying. The prices used in a restaurant must provide a perceived value to customers because they decide whether or not they are receiving their money's worth.

Premium Pricing as a Strategy

Because customers have expectations of value for their money, pricing can help a restaurant achieve the desired premium position or high competitive position in the market. Selling products or services at a high price can create prestige or a premium position. Research has shown that consumers associate higher prices with higher quality offerings. The premium position can be supported by exquisite attention to detail (see *Exhibit 4d*):

Exhibit 4d

Elegant décor and high quality food and service support a restaurant's premium pricing.

■ The décor is elegant and spotlessly clean.

■ The menu is printed on high-quality paper that reflects the décor.

■ Service is performed excellently by a well-trained staff.

■ The highest quality food products are purchased and then prepared by a well-trained staff.

■ The menu may offer a unique or specialty item for which there is no comparison.

In other words, the prices are reflective of the premium position. This position can be supported if there is a sufficiently large market segment that will appreciate this kind of quality and, more important, be willing to pay for it. Restaurant managers should do market research to determine whether this is true.

Exhibit 4e

These prices are consistent with this restaurant's competition.

Competitive Pricing as a Strategy

Competitive pricing is another strategy that can be used to position a restaurant or brand in the market. In this situation, a restaurant has identified other restaurants with which it intends to compete and, through research, has defined the wants and needs of a similar market segment.

The pricing structure for menu offerings is based on competitors' pricing structures because similar customers' demands are being met. (See *Exhibit 4e*.) It is necessary to be aware of competition's prices, but to be effective, the restaurants must have a similar cost structure.

Be aware—a competitive position in the market is not established only by pricing. As in premium positioning, the décor, food quality, portion size, and service are all perceived by the customer as being part of the price. To remain competitive and profitable, the restaurant has to provide the product and service as well, as or better than, the competition at a lower or similar cost.

Use of Price in Market Segmentation

Another approach to pricing is to further refine the markets into smaller groups with similar wants and needs. This practice is defined as **market segmentation.** As in premium pricing or competitive pricing, a market has to be identified for the goods and services provided. Typical market segments for restaurants include (see *Exhibit 4f*):

- Senior citizens
- Small children
- Teenagers
- Family
- Happy hour

Senior Citizens

Senior citizens are an important market segment, and this segment will continue to grow as the U.S. population ages. In general, the senior citizen market tends to be value conscious. Their needs might be met by offering smaller portions with a correspondingly lower price. Meeting their needs might also include offering some healthier items that are lower in fat and calories. Dinner specials for seniors could be offered earlier in the dinner hour to increase sales during what might otherwise be a slow time, since many seniors prefer to dine early. On the other hand, if your target market includes senior citizens, be sure to research their needs before making any decisions. Many seniors are affluent with disposable income to spend.

Exhibit 4f

Market Segmentation

Senior citizens

Small children

Teenagers

Family

Happy hour

Small Children

Another important market segment to consider is small children because, in many cases, they help make family dining decisions. A restaurant that offers a children's menu is inviting families to its operation. A menu developed for children should offer small portions of familiar food items. The menu should provide some variety, but not be too large or confusing. Again, a lower price can be charged because of the smaller portions. Many children's menus are offered separately from the regular menu because the children's menu provides activities for children to engage in while waiting for their food. Other advantages of the children's menu are allowing children to select their own food, increasing the check, and preventing parents from sharing their plates with children.

Teenagers

Teenagers make up another target market with special demands. Active, growing teenagers tend to require larger amounts of food. They are often very busy and do not have much time to eat a meal. One technique used to target teenagers is the concept of **product-bundle pricing,** or combining several products and offering them at a price lower than the price would be if they were sold individually. Some very competitive quick-service restaurants offer value or combination meals in which several items are bundled or offered for one price, and can also be served quickly. Many of these meals include a choice of healthier food, such as fresh fruit instead of French fries, and milk or bottled water in place of carbonated beverages.

Family

Some restaurants have defined a family market segment that meets the demands of families by offering meals at a reasonable price. Often in this market, one family member picks up the meal and takes it home for dinner. It meets the family's desire to have dinner together while saving time on preparation. Another way these needs can be met is to provide family-style service in a restaurant at a competitive price.

Happy Hour

Happy hour menus may be designed to meet the needs of the singles market segment. The demands of this group often include the opportunity to socialize. Providing beverages and appetizers at a low price gives them a chance to relax and socialize after work. Since happy hours are usually held in the early evening, it is another opportunity for a restaurant to increase sales at a time that might not otherwise be busy.

Activity

Demands for Different Market Segments

For each of the market segments listed below, describe the demands placed on the restaurant and its menu.

1 Business lunch: _____

2 Pre-work (commuter) breakfast: _____

3 Fine dining: _____

4 Party and banquet: _____

5 Carry-out: _____

6 Off-site catering: _____

7 Sports event special (e.g., Super Bowl): _____

8 Dine-in holiday: _____

9 Catered holiday: _____

Pricing and Gross Profit Margin

In the determination of profitability, gross profit margin plays a large role. In its simplest form, **gross profit margin** is the money remaining after the cost of goods sold has been subtracted from total sales.

Total sales − Cost of goods = Gross profit margin

The gross profit margin is a figure found on an income statement. (See *Exhibit 4g.*) This section will relate gross profit margin to menu items and their prices.

Exhibit 4g

Sample Income Statement

Statement of Income for Sally's Steaks
January 1, 2008—December 31, 2008

	Amount	Sales %
Sales		
Food	$. 75,000	75.0%
Beverage	25,000	25.0%
Total sales	$100,000	100.0%
Cost of Goods Sold		
Food	$. 27,000	27.0%
Beverage	6,000	6.0%
Total cost of goods sold	$. 33,000	33.0%
Gross Profit		
Total gross profit	$. 67,000	67.0%
Direct Labor		
Total labor	$. 34,000	34.0%
Other Controllable Expenses		
Employee benefits	$. . 2,600	2.6%
Management salaries	3,000	3.0%
Employee meals	400	0.4%
Accrued vacations and holidays	500	0.5%
Supplies	1,000	1.0%
Replacement china and flatware	400	0.4%
Linen rental	300	0.3%
Utilities	1,100	1.1%
Cleaning and sanitation	700	0.7%
Repairs and maintenance	900	0.9%
Advertising	800	0.8%
Music and entertainment	300	0.3%
Total other controllable expenses	$. 12,000	12.0%
Noncontrollable Expenses		
Rent	$. . 6,100	6.1%
Insurance	2,200	2.2%
Property taxes	2,300	2.3%
Interest	600	0.6%
Depreciation	2,800	2.8%
Total noncontrollable expenses	$. 14,000	14.0%
Total expenses	$60,000	60.0%
Income before taxes	$. 7,000	7.0%
Taxes	$. 2,000	
Net income	$. 5,000	

Think About It...

Gross profit can also be expressed as a percentage of total sales, in which case it is called the gross profit margin ratio. Similar ratios can be made for food cost, labor cost, and other costs.

Gross Profit Margin and the Income Statement

An income statement—also known as a profit and loss statement—is an accounting report of the revenues taken in and the expenses incurred in different categories by an organization during a certain time period. If money is left over, then it is called a net profit. If expenses are greater than revenues, then there is a net loss.

On an income statement, the first entry is the revenue, or sales dollars. The sales dollar amount is the sum of the prices charged for all menu items sold during the time period covered by the income statement. The cost of goods sold—also known as the cost of food sold or simply food cost—appears as the first subtraction from sales on the statement. The gross profit margin—also known simply as gross profit—is the amount of income remaining after subtracting food cost from sales.

Gross profit dollars are used to pay for the operational expenses of the organization and, hopefully, leave some profit afterward. Operating expenses include controllable costs such as labor, utilities, and advertising, and noncontrollable costs such as rent and insurance.

An alternative way of describing the gross profit margin is the amount of money customers pay for the services provided by a restaurant beyond the cost of the food itself. These include the costs of purchasing, preparing, and cooking the food, delivering the food to the customer, cleaning up afterward, and maintaining the facility and its furnishings. Customers who cook at home and do their own cleanup still have to pay for the food they buy at the grocery store. Therefore, the cost of the service provided above the cost of the food can be considered the gross profit margin.

Gross Profit Margin of a Menu Item

Each menu item has a gross profit margin. You can think of each menu item similarly to the income statement for the operation. This has been done in *Exhibit 4h*.

■ The menu item price is equivalent to the total sales.

■ The food cost of the item is equivalent to the cost of goods sold.

■ The gross profit of the item is equivalent to the overall gross profit.

■ A portion of the overall operating costs belongs to the item.

■ A portion of the overall profit belongs to the item.

Therefore, a menu item's price can be calculated with the following formula:

Food cost + Gross profit margin = Menu item's price

In this formula, the gross profit margin is the element that can change; the cost of the food is a given. If the price charged for the item is greater than the food cost, the gross profit margin will be positive, and selling the item will contribute those dollars to the operation. If the price charged for the item is lower than the food cost, the gross profit margin will be negative and that item will be sold at a loss.

Exhibit 4h

Comparison of the Income Statement to Menu Price

Simplified Income Statement			Menu Price Breakdown		
	Amount	Sales %		Amount	Sales %
Total sales	$100,000	(100%)	Price	$10.00	(100%)
Less cost of goods sold	−33,000	(33%)	Food cost	−3.30	(33%)
Gross profit	$ 67,000	(67%)	Gross profit	$ 6.70	(67%)
Less labor cost	−34,000	(34%)	Labor cost	−3.40	(34%)
Less other controllable expenses	−12,000	(12%)	Expenses (controllable)	−1.20	(12%)
Less noncontrollable expenses	−14,000	(14%)	Expenses (noncontrollable)	−1.40	(14%)
Total expenses	−60,000	(60%)	Total expenses	−6.00	(60%)
Pre tax profit	$ 7,000	(7%)	Profit	$ 0.70	(7%)

Pricing Methods

There are many methods of pricing menu items. These methods vary from just pricing the same as the competition, to some that consider costs, to some that are very complex. Four of the basic methods will be presented in this section.

Some of these methods work only for entrées or other items with a large dollar price. That is because these methods add a calculated dollar amount to the food cost to arrive at a menu price. Obviously, adding the same dollar amount to all categories of menu items—for example, beverages—would result in ridiculously high prices for items that should have a low price. Using beverages again as an example—it would be silly to add a fixed five-dollar amount to a cup of coffee costing two cents for a menu price of $5.02. Consequently, other methods must be used for certain menu items.

In fact, some experts argue that using any one pricing method for the entire menu is illogical. It is recommended that different methods be used for different categories of menu items. In addition, all the methods explained below result in a mathematical menu price. This price should almost never be used. Rather, menu prices must always be adjusted to take into account pricing psychology, the restaurant's market segment, the area of the country, the time of year, etc.

Food Cost Percentage Method

In the **food cost percentage** method, you set the percentage of menu price that the food cost must be, and then calculate the price that will provide this percentage using the following formula:

Item food cost ÷ Food cost percentage = Menu price

Determining the Food Cost Percentage

The food cost percentage is the result of dividing the total food cost (cost of goods sold) by total sales.

Total food cost ÷ Total sales = Food cost percentage

Using the figures from the sample income statement in *Exhibit 4g* on p. 71, where total sales are $100,000 and cost of goods sold (total food cost) is $33,000, the calculation of food cost percentage is as follows:

$33,000 ÷ $100,000 = .33 or 33%

Calculating the Food Cost

In calculating the menu price, you may use either the current actual food cost percentage (calculated above) or a target food cost percentage. You would use a higher target percentage if you thought the calculated one was too low.

You also must know the food cost of each menu item, and this food cost must be the entire food cost of the menu item. For example, if the price being determined is for a steak entrée that includes a baked potato with sour cream, tossed salad with dressing, and onion ring garnish, then the cost of each item has to be included in the item food cost. (See *Exhibit 4i.*)

Exhibit 4i

Food Cost Example of Steak Entrée

Steak $3.83

Baked potato 0.49

Sour cream 0.22

Tossed salad 0.52

Dressing 0.41

Onion ring garnish . . 0.39

Total $5.86

Calculating the Menu Price

Once the food cost of the item is known and the desired food cost percentage has been identified, the price of the menu item is determined by dividing the item food cost by the food cost percentage.

Item food cost ÷ Food cost percentage = Menu price

For example, since the targeted food cost percentage is 33 percent, and the total food cost for the steak entrée is $5.86, the calculation is as follows:

$5.86 ÷ 0.33 = $17.76

This is the mathematical price—the one obtained by mathematical calculation of the menu item. The price that will be put on the menu should reflect pricing psychology, consideration of the restaurant market, and what the customer is willing to pay. The price could be set at $17.95 in a competitive market, or at $18 in a premium market.

Activity

Determine Menu Price Using the Food Cost Percentage Method

The owner of Sally's Steaks wants to add a new chicken dish to the menu in response to customer requests. She has determined that the food cost of the proposed menu item, including all the side items, is $4.93. Her current food cost percentage is 34%. Using the food cost percentage method, determine the mathematical menu price for the new chicken entrée, then suggest an actual menu price.

■ Mathematical price _____

■ Actual menu price _____

Pros and Cons of Food Cost Percentage Method

Because food cost percentage is dependent on the costs of the food and its preparation within the foodservice operation, an accurate food cost percentage will be different for each menu category: appetizers, salads, entrées, featured dishes, desserts, beverages, liquors, etc. Therefore, using the same food cost percentage for all categories of menu items is not logical. Many restaurants that use the food percentage method have different food cost percentages for each menu category.

Average Check Method

The average check method can only be used by an established restaurant. In this method, the average amount of money spent by customers is used to determine a price category. Then all prices are set to fit into this category. The average check is determined for a specific period of time, such as a month. The basic formula for the average check method is:

Total revenue ÷ Number of checks = Average check

Average Check While Estimating the Number of Customers

Most foodservice operations do not keep an accurate count of the number of checks or the number of customers. Therefore, there is an alternate formula using data that is readily available in a restaurant. This formula is a little more complicated and requires several items of information:

- Length of the time period to use

- Total revenue for the specified period

- Number of seats in the restaurant

- Average turnover of those seats

- Number of days the restaurant is open in the specified period, such as thirty days in a month

The last three items are used to estimate the number of checks. The practical formula for average check is:

$$\frac{\text{Total revenue}}{\text{Number of seats} \times \text{Average turnover} \times \text{Number of days open}} = \text{Average check}$$

Here is an example of an average check calculation. Say that you manage a restaurant that has the following data: the total revenue for the month is $100,000, the number of seats is 175, the average seat turnover is 1.5 times per day, and the restaurant is open 30 days in the average month. Therefore, the average check is:

$$\frac{\$100{,}000}{175 \times 1.5 \times 30} = \$12.70$$

Variations by Meal Period

In the above example, it was assumed that the restaurant has the same average check at every meal. If the restaurant serves breakfast, lunch, and dinner, there may be a different average check for each meal period. In this case, it would be necessary to determine the revenue and turnover for each meal separately. Then a more accurate check average could be determined for each meal.

Determining the Menu Prices

Once the average check figure has been determined, the price range for all menu items must be determined. Then the prices of menu items can be established within the identified price range.

In the previous example, the average check was found to be $12.70, which can be used to establish the price range for the restaurant. The price range for each menu item could be set from $10.00 to $15.00. The actual prices would vary according to pricing psychology and might be written as $10.95, $10.99, or $11.00, depending on the market.

Activity

Determine Menu Prices Using the Average Check Method

Sally's Steaks has a total revenue of $250,000 for a month. There are 200 seats in the dining room with an average turnover of 2.5 times per day. The restaurant is open thirty days in the month. Find the average check and set a price range for menu items.

1 Average check _____

2 Price range _____

Contribution Margin Method

This is a pricing method that works only for entrées and other major menu items. The **contribution margin** method uses operation-wide data to determine a dollar amount that must be added to each major menu item's food cost. A foodservice operation can use the same contribution margin for all its menu items, or it can calculate separate contribution margins for different menu categories. There are two versions of the formula:

Contribution margin $+$ **Food cost** $=$ **Menu price**

$$\frac{\textbf{Total nonfood cost} + \textbf{Target profit}}{\textbf{Number of customers}} + \textbf{Food cost} = \textbf{Menu price}$$

You can see that in the first formula, the first term is the contribution margin.

Think About It...

In a profitable restaurant, each menu item must contribute a dollar amount to the running of the foodservice operation. Thus, the item's price can be calculated as the cost of the item's food plus a dollar amount called the item's contribution margin. This is the contribution margin method of pricing.

Food cost + Contribution margin = Menu price

This formula is the same as the formula for gross profit. In the foodservice industry, gross profit is also known as the contribution margin.

The contribution margin is the combination of nonfood costs and profit.

Nonfood cost + Profit = Contribution margin

Therefore, the menu price formula can be rewritten as the following:

$$\Big(\text{ Nonfood cost } + \text{ Profit }\Big) + \text{ Food cost } = \text{ Menu price}$$

Generally, a foodservice operation does not know the cost of nonfood factors (e.g., rent, utilities, labor, etc.) of an individual menu item, nor does it know the profit for an individual item. Therefore, these amounts have to be derived from the total nonfood costs and the total profit of the entire operation. The most available data is in terms of the number of entrées ordered or the number of customers. Therefore, an average of these amounts on a per-customer basis can be determined; this is shown in the following equation as the second element.

$$\text{Food cost} + \frac{\text{Total nonfood cost } + \text{ Target profit}}{\text{Number of customers}} = \text{Menu price}$$

The contribution margin method of pricing depends upon very accurate accounting procedures and consistent customer counts. It has the advantage of considering all the costs of operation and profit in the pricing method. However, the costs of operation are spread over all the customers; if a large drop in customers occurred, these costs would not be covered.

Determining the Contribution Margin and the Menu Price

To use the contribution margin method, you must have all the required data for the same time period. The nonfood costs may be newly calculated or taken from a recent profit and loss (income) statement. The profit that appears on this statement may be used as the target profit if it is sufficient; otherwise, a higher profit should be used.

Here is an example for determining these figures. Continuing with the data from *Exhibit 4g* on p. 73, the operating costs for a certain period are $60,000, the target profit for the same period is $7,000, the sales volume for the same period is 10,000 customers, and the food costs for the item are $5.86.

The calculation of the menu price using the contribution margin method is as follows:

$$\$5.86 \; + \; \frac{\$60,000 \; + \; \$7,000}{10,000} \; = \; \textbf{Menu price}$$

$$\$5.86 \; + \; \$6.70 \; = \; \$12.56$$

The mathematical menu price has been determined to be $12.56. Again, pricing psychology, the restaurant's market, and what the customer is willing to pay must be considered in setting the menu price—for example, $12.75 or $12.95.

Determining the Menu Price of Another Item

To determine the menu price of another item, such as one with a food cost of $4.27, add the same contribution margin to its food cost.

$$\textbf{Food cost} \; + \; \textbf{Contribution margin} \; = \; \textbf{Menu price}$$

$$\$6.70 \; + \; \$4.27 \; = \; \$10.97$$

Activity

Determine the Menu Price Using the Contribution Margin Method

The owner of Sally's Steaks has determined that her operating costs were $125,000 for last month. The targeted profit is $15,000. The sales volume for last month was 17,500 customers. The food cost of the menu item she is trying to price is $4.93. Find the mathematical menu price for the menu item using the contribution margin (also known as gross profit) method and suggest an actual menu price.

1 Mathematical price _____

2 Actual menu price _____

Straight Markup Pricing Method

Although they are mathematically related, markup is different from a margin. A margin is thought of in terms of the selling price; a markup is thought of in terms of the cost. Straight markup pricing refers to a pricing method in which the selling price is obtained by marking up the costs according to a formula. The selling price obtained is the mathematical price; the actual menu price should reflect a good application of pricing psychology.

Ideally, the dollar amount of the markup should be large enough to cover the operating costs of the foodservice operation and include a reasonable profit; however, this is not a requirement. An underlying assumption of this method is that each customer will help pay for labor, operating costs, and the cost of food, as well as contribute to profit.

There are two variations on the straight markup pricing method: adding a set dollar amount markup to the food cost, or adding a percentage markup to the food cost.

Set Dollar Amount Markup Method

This method is another one that works only for major menu items. The set dollar amount markup method simply adds a fixed dollar amount to the food cost of an item. In order to utilize this method, you must know the food cost and the dollar amount of the markup.

Food cost + Markup = Menu price

First, the dollar markup is calculated. This can be broken down into separate **profit, labor,** and **operating cost** markups.

$$\text{Profit per menu item} + \text{Labor cost per menu item} + \text{Operating cost per menu item} = \text{Markup}$$

To determine the desired profit per menu item, the restaurant must first determine the desired profit dollars, and then average this amount over the total number of customers. For example, a restaurant would like to make $10,000 per month in profit. If the average number of customers per month is 10,000, then the profit required from each customer is $1.00.

To determine the desired labor cost per menu item, the restaurant must first determine the total labor dollars, and then average this amount over the total number of customers. If the labor costs for a month are $34,000, and there are 10,000 customers, then the labor cost per customer is $3.40.

To determine the operating cost per menu item, the restaurant must first determine the total operating cost, and then average this amount over the total number of customers. The operating costs for the same month are $26,000. The average operating cost per customer is then found by dividing $26,000 by 10,000 customers to yield an operating cost per customer of $2.60.

The markup is the sum of these three amounts.

$1.00 + $3.40 + $2.60 = $7.00

To determine the mathematical menu price for each item, add the markup to the food cost of each menu item. If the food cost of the item is $5.86, then the menu price is calculated like this:

$5.86 + $7.00 = $12.86

The mathematical price is $12.86. Using pricing psychology, the restaurant's market position, and the amount the customer is willing to pay, the menu price might be set at $12.95.

Set Percentage Increase Method

The set percentage increase method builds on the set dollar amount markup method and takes it a step further. By doing this, you get a percentage that is more general and avoids the problems with adding a fixed dollar amount to each entrée food cost.

Basically, you calculate the markup as shown previously for one or several menu items. Then you determine what percentage markup these dollars are in comparison to the items' food costs.

Food cost × Percentage = Markup

Markup ÷ Food cost = Percentage

Using the markup and food costs from the set dollar amount markup method example allows you to calculate a percentage markup for all menu items.

$7.00 ÷ $5.86 = 119%

This means that a markup equal to 119 percent of the food cost of each menu item should be added to the food cost to get the menu price. If the food cost of another menu item is $4.27, then the markup would be 119 percent of $4.27, or $5.08.

Remember that the menu price is the sum of the markup and the food cost.

So the menu price of this item is given by the following formula:

$4.27 + $5.08 = $9.35

Another way to calculate the menu price with a percentage markup is by multiplying the food cost by a total markup percentage. You can see the relationship between the fixed dollar markup and the percentage multiplier in the following series of formulas:

Food cost + Markup = Menu price

Food cost + (Food cost × Percentage) = Menu price

Food cost + (1 + Percentage) = Menu price

Food cost + (100% + Percentage) = Menu price

Using the previous example, where the food cost is $4.27 and the markup percentage is 119 percent, produces this calculation:

Food cost + (100% + Percentage) = Menu price

$4.27 + (100% + 119%) = $9.35

$4.27 + 219% = $9.35

The 219 percent could have been written as a multiplier of 2.19, which means that the food cost is increased 2.19 times to get the mathematical menu price. This multiplier is also called a **markup factor.**

Remember that these menu prices are merely the mathematically calculated menu prices. The actual menu price considers pricing psychology, the restaurant's market position, and how much the customers will pay. So the actual menu price for this item might be $9.95, or perhaps $9.50.

The straight markup percentage method has the advantage of being very easy to use once the factor is determined. A drawback to the method is that it establishes a food cost percentage before the food is purchased, stored, or cooked. In reality, the food cost percentage varies over time due to increased costs of food, food that is not properly stored or cooked and may have to be discarded, etc. The other caution is to consider that other costs of operation, such as labor, are not really considered in this method. Some restaurants use a different markup for each category of food offered on the menu to account for increased labor costs that might be applicable to certain categories.

Activity

Determine the Menu Price Using the Straight Markup Percentage Method

The owner of Sally's Steaks has decided to establish 233% as the markup percentage that will be used to price menu items. The cost of the menu item she wants to price is $4.93. Find the menu price for the item using the straight markup percentage method.

1 Mathematical price _____

2 Actual menu price _____

Employee Meal Pricing

If providing meals to employees is a benefit provided by the foodservice operation, then the cost of the food used must be accounted for in order to maintain accurate food costs. There are two methods in common use:

1. Different food for employees

2. Dollar value of food for employees

Different Food for Employees

One method of accounting for this cost of food is to provide meals for the employees that are different from the menu items offered to customers. Then the actual cost of the food can be easily identified because it has been kept separate from other food costs.

Dollar Value of Food for Employees

If employees select food from the regular menu, the costs of food can be identified in two ways:

1. Assign a fixed dollar amount for each employee meal. The total of the fixed amount per meal, multiplied by the number of employees, is the cost of food for employee meals. For example, for employee dinners, assume a food cost of $5.00. If ten employees eat dinner, the total employee food cost is $50.00.

2. Have the employees order food through the regular ordering system with a special code that identifies the order as an employee meal. Then the actual food costs of each item ordered can be identified.

The second method would be more accurate in accounting for employee food costs, but it requires that the point-of-sale (POS) system be programmed to provide the necessary information.

Summary

Price is an important part of the strategic marketing plan for a restaurant. It serves the purpose of determining profitability and providing information to the customer. Price has an important role in brand positioning, setting pricing objectives, and achieving the intended gross profit margin. The external environment, from the local competition to global events, is important to consider when pricing menus.

Price can be used to differentiate a competitive strategy from a premium pricing strategy. Consumers are sensitive to price and expect value for the money spent in a restaurant. The market can be segmented into specific market segments or target markets using pricing strategies.

Four basic pricing methods are used to determine menu prices: the food cost percentage method, the average check method, the contribution margin method, and the straight markup pricing method using a dollar amount or a percentage.

Ways to account for employee meals include providing different food for employees, assigning a fixed dollar amount for each employee meal, and accounting for employee meal food cost using the restaurant in-house ordering system.

Review Your Learning

1 The objective of status quo pricing is to

A. maximize profit in the long term.

B. maintain a competitive position in the marketplace.

C. maintain prices at the same level no matter what happens.

D. emphasize sales volume and not profit.

2 Using the food cost percentage pricing method and the following information, what will the menu price most likely be? The food cost percentage is 29 percent and the food cost of the menu item is $5.17.

A. $15.95

B. $11.50

C. $13.45

D. $17.95

3 If an orange crop is destroyed by severe storms, what could be one possible effect on a restaurant?

A. The supply of orange juice will increase and the price will go up.

B. The supply of orange juice will increase and the price will go down.

C. The supply of orange juice will decrease and the price will go up.

D. The supply of orange juice will decrease and the price will go down.

4 Some customers are likely to respond to price cuts in menu prices by

A. not paying attention to them and thinking that they just got lucky.

B. wondering if something is wrong with the food quality or service.

C. insisting on paying full price anyway.

D. adding extra money to the server's tip to keep it the same as before.

5 The concept of product-bundle pricing is

A. combining several menu items as a group for a reduced price.

B. not a good idea for the restaurant industry because it reduces profits.

C. a way to make the most money from a group of food items.

D. often targeted to seniors.

6 The gross profit method of determining menu prices uses operational costs of $75,000, a target profit of 8 percent or $13,000, a sales volume of 11,000 customers, and a food cost of a menu item of $6.12. What is the mathematical menu price most likely to be?

A. $17.12

B. $14.25

C. $7.65

D. $14.12

7 A premium pricing strategy for a restaurant would be reinforced through the use of

A. "Buy one entrée and get one entrée free" offers.

B. bright orange walls, loud music, and servers with no training.

C. well-trained servers and cooks and specialty food items.

D. menu prices that are set way below those of the competition.

8 The best menu for the children's market segment would

A. provide limited offerings, familiar food items, and an activity.

B. be as extensive as the restaurant menu but with reduced prices.

C. be part of the elegant restaurant menu.

D. offer foie gras and Brussels sprouts at reduced prices because they do not sell well.

Notes

The Alcoholic Beverage Menu

5

Inside This Chapter

- Alcoholic Beverages in Restaurants
- Merchandising Wine
- Merchandising Spirits
- Merchandising Beers and Ales
- Pricing Alcoholic Beverages

After completing this chapter, you should be able to:

- Identify and list ways to present a liquor menu.
- List and describe typical elements of wine and spirits lists and the methods used to merchandise them.
- Categorize and describe spirits, beers, ales, liqueurs, and cordials.
- Price the beverage menu.

Test Your Knowledge

1. **True or False:** A good wine-food pairing suggestion is to offer a dry white wine with a beef entrée. *(See p. 89.)*

2. **True or False:** In the United States, liqueurs are also known as cordials. *(See p. 93.)*

3. **True or False:** It does not matter to the customer what kind of glass brandy is served in as long as the brandy is of the desired quality. *(See p. 94.)*

4. **True or False:** Most beer can be defined as either lager or ale. *(See p. 94.)*

5. **True or False:** If the markup standard on bottles of wine is one hundred percent in the restaurant, then all bottles of wine should be marked up one hundred percent. *(See p. 96.)*

Key Terms

Ale	Grain spirits	Set loss
Bitters	Hops	Sommelier
Bock beer	Lager	Spirits
Brandy	Liqueur	Standard pour
Call brand	Malt	Stout
Call liquor	Malt liquor	Varietal wine
Cordial	Must	Vintner
Distilled spirits	Plant liquors	Wheat beer
Draft beer	Porter	Wine
Generic wine	Proof	Yeast

Introduction

Offering alcoholic beverages to customers is an integral part of the dining experience at many restaurants. Many customers regard it as an enjoyable accompaniment to their food. If it is in keeping with the character of the establishment, pairing items from the food and alcoholic beverage menus that complement each other can enhance customers' dining and drinking experience. (See *Exhibit 5a.*) Offering alcoholic beverage service also plays a very important role in the profitability of an operation, so it comes as no surprise that many restaurants want to offer alcoholic beverage service to their guests.

Meeting the needs and expectations of customers is just as important to your alcoholic beverage service as it is to the selection of food menu offerings. Depending on the focus of the operation, the alcoholic beverage menu may be limited or extensive, and can be provided to the customer in a variety of ways.

Since alcoholic beverage service makes such a strong contribution to the operation's profit margin, it is important that your staff is well trained and knowledgeable about the beverages you offer. They need to be able to categorize, describe, and recommend various spirits, beers, ales, liqueurs, cordials, and wines to customers in order to increase sales where appropriate.

The presentation of the liquor menu and the design of the wine and spirits lists are important tools to use when merchandising alcoholic beverages. In this chapter, the different types of alcoholic beverages will be explained, as well as strategies and techniques for marketing and pricing the products.

Exhibit 5a

Serving alcohol beverages contributes to the dining experience of customers as well as to the restaurant's profits.

Alcoholic Beverages in Restaurants

The main categories of alcoholic beverages that might be served in a restaurant are spirits, wine, and beer. The defining feature among the three categories is the percentage of alcohol content in each of them. Another major difference can be found in their different methods of production. These categories will be discussed in turn as they are examined for:

- Beverage types in each product group and their individual characteristics

- Specifics of merchandising

- Mechanics and details of pricing

Serving Alcoholic Beverages Increases Profits

The average markup for alcoholic beverages typically falls between 300 and 400 percent, while food items are given a much lower markup—between 100 and 200 percent. Consequently, this substantially higher markup generates gross margin and net profit figures that are much greater than food items. In addition, when customers order alcoholic beverages, it is reflected in an increase in the total check. The net result for the restaurant is greater revenues and higher profits.

Laws Restricting Alcohol Service

While merchandising alcoholic beverages within the restaurant often leads to higher profits, it is important to remember that there are regulations unique to each of the fifty states that must be observed when serving alcohol. Additionally, local and municipal liquor commissions can impose their own codes and regulations on top of those legislated by state law. The regulations control both the sale and service of alcohol. It is the responsibility of the restaurant to adhere to these regulations and control patrons' access to alcohol. All restaurants should have identification carding programs designed to verify that patrons are of legal age to drink. (See *Exhibit 5b.*)

Exhibit 5b

Example of identification carding program

Appears with permission from the
Illinois Liquor Control Commission

The types of alcoholic beverages served in a particular restaurant depend on the type of liquor license issued to the establishment, the customers' expectations, the types of food offered, the brand image, and the restaurant's costs. Most states separate liquor licenses into different categories:

■ Beer only

■ Beer and wine

■ Beer, wine, and spirits

The categorizations in your state may differ.

Because of increased control over the sale and service of alcohol, alcoholic beverages are usually considered as a complement to the food menu offerings in a restaurant, unlike in a bar or tavern where they are the primary menu offerings.

Liquor Menus

An important role of the liquor menu is to make customers aware that the establishment serves alcoholic beverages. The alcoholic beverages offered and the look of the liquor menu should support the theme of the restaurant or type of food offered there. Alcoholic beverages may be included on the food menu if they are few in number. Sometimes they are listed on a separate page; in other instances, they are listed in a separate section. It is recommended that space on the food menu be used to offer house-specialty alcoholic beverages that are profitable.

An alcoholic beverages-only menu can be used if the restaurant wants to merchandise a larger selection of alcoholic beverages, in which case it is recommended that the most profitable house specialties are featured and positioned prominently. If the wine inventory is very small, a few featured bottles of wine might make up a display in the dining room or occupy a set-off block on the food menu. If there is a more extensive wine inventory, a separate wine list is a good way to merchandise wines. If the restaurant wants to merchandise beer on a menu, the available beers are usually listed with draft beer separated from bottled beer and domestic from imported beer.

Think About It...

According to a USDA 2003 report, in the United States in 2001, per capita consumption of beer was 21.7 gallons. The average person also drank 2.0 gallons of wine and 1.3 gallons of distilled spirits.

Merchandising Wine

Wines are effectively merchandised when they are listed conveniently and served well. Some restaurants with extensive wine selections use a **sommelier**—the French term for the wine steward or the person responsible for wine in a restaurant—to suggest and serve wines to guests.

The wine category includes table wines, fortified wines, apéritifs, dessert wines, and sparkling wines.

- **Table wines** include red, white, and blush wines (also known as rosé wines). They are traditionally served with food during a meal. The alcohol content of table wines in the United States varies from about 11 percent to no higher than 14 percent.

- **Fortified wines** are higher in alcohol content—14 to 24 percent—and sweeter than table wines. They are created by adding extra alcohol from a spirit, such as brandy, to a wine during fermentation.

- **Apéritif wines** are served before meals as an appetizer and are often fortified and herb-flavored.

- **Dessert wines** are served after dinner as a dessert or with desserts. These wines are also fortified, but even sweeter than fortified wines.

- **Sparkling wines** contain 13 to 14 percent alcohol plus bubbles of carbon dioxide; common examples are champagne and Asti Spumante.

Wine is made from the fermentation of grapes. Fermentation is the process by which alcohol is created through the breakdown of sugars by yeast into alcohol and carbon dioxide. There are many kinds of grapes from which wine is made. (See *Exhibit 5c* on the next page.)

Exhibit 5c

The type of grapes and the winemaking process contribute to the flavors and colors of wine.

Red wines are made from red or black grapes. White wines are made from white grapes, but can be made from red grapes if the skins are separated from the juice right after pressing. If wines are made from just one type of grape, they are called **varietal wines,** such as Chardonnay or Merlot. If wines are made from a blend of wines, they are called **generic wines,** often representing a wine-growing region such as Bordeaux.

The overall process of producing wine involves the following steps:

1 After harvest, the grapes are washed and pressed gently to release the juice, or **must.**

2 The must is fermented by naturally occurring yeasts from the grape skins. Wines are fermented at different temperatures until the yeast uses up the natural sugars or the alcohol content reaches approximately 14 percent. Red wines are usually fermented at higher temperatures than white wines.

3 The wine is aged in wooden or metal barrels for a specific number of years. During the aging period, wine is sampled and the quality is judged.

4 When the wine has developed sufficiently, it is bottled.

Factors that contribute to the different flavors and colors of wine include:

- Type of grape or grapes used

- Pressing process

- Fermentation

- Type and length of the aging process

- Area or region where grapes were produced

- Year in which grapes were produced

- Vintner responsible for production

Because wines have different flavors and colors, different wines are more appropriately served with particular types of food. For example:

- Beef entrées are complemented by hearty red wines such as Bordeaux, Cabernet Sauvignon, or Pinot Noir.

- Seafood is enhanced by dry or fairly dry white wines such as Chardonnay or Sauvignon Blanc.

Exhibit 5d

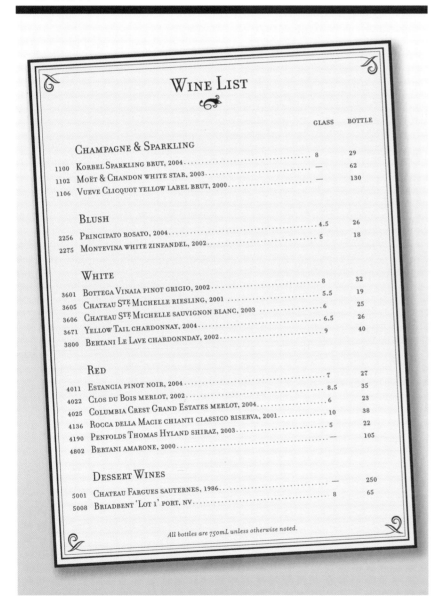

Wine list by the bottle and the glass

- Poultry goes well with full-bodied white wines such as Chardonnay or Chablis.

- Fruity desserts are complemented by a sweet white table wine or champagne.

- Chocolate desserts are good with a sweet red wine such as Valpolicella.

There are many more possible food and wine pairings. Additionally, customers may have their own ideas of which wines they prefer to drink with certain types of food.

Designing the Wine List

In designing a wine list (see *Exhibit 5d*), some decisions have to be made about the wines that will be offered. Those decisions need to be made within the context of the brand image of the restaurant, the type of dining being offered, the customers' expectations, and the types of food appearing on the menu.

Another decision concerns whether wines will be offered and priced by the glass, the bottle, or some combination of both. Yet another decision is how extensive a wine list to offer: just a few choices, several dozen choices, or hundreds of choices. Once these decisions have been made, the design of the wine list can begin; however, a good wine list is difficult to prepare unless the author has an extensive knowledge of wines.

The wines can be listed on the menu if the list of choices is fairly short, or a separate wine list can be offered if the selection of wines is more extensive. On the wine list, it is helpful to present the different kinds of wine under appropriate headings, such as apéritifs, red wines, sparkling wines, and so forth. Wines are often listed by year, **vintner** (winery), name of wine, and the state (in the United States), region, or country from which they come. Some wine lists include short descriptions of the wines, and some offer serving suggestions that pair the wine with specifically chosen menu items.

There is no single correct way to prepare a wine list; instead, there are a variety of ways. There are even model wine lists available. Your wine distributor can also be helpful. Your choices will depend on what you wish to emphasize or what you think your customers will want to know.

The wine list is usually alphabetized within a category, so the first item in each entry should be the term that you want used for alphabetizing. Many wine lists are organized according to key information about the wines carried. In some of these lists, the information is the same, but the sequence appears to be a matter of judgment. Common variations are:

- Year, vintner, variety, geography, price

- Variety, vintner, geography, year, price

- Vintner, variety, geography, year, price

- Vintner, variety, year, geography, price

An example of these four listing choices is shown in *Exhibit 5e.*

Exhibit 5e

Wine List Alternatives

2000, St. Supéry, Sauvignon Blanc, Napa Valley, California, $22

-or-

Sauvignon Blanc, St. Supéry, Napa Valley, California, 2000, $22

-or-

St. Supéry, Sauvignon Blanc, Napa Valley, California, 2000, $22
This wine is recommended with white fish, such as cod or bass.

-or-

St. Supéry, Sauvignon Blanc, 2000, Napa Valley, California, $22
This wine is recommended with our Skewered Shrimp entrée

There is also variation in the way to describe the wine. Which type and the amount of description you use depends on the information your customers are likely to need. You can include the following additional information (see *Exhibit 5e*):

- ■ Basic information regarding variety, vintner, geography, year, and price

- ■ Description of the wine's flavor

- ■ Description of broad food categories that go well with the wine, such as beef, poultry, fish, etc.

- ■ Description of particular dishes or specific food preparations the wine complements.

Serving Wine

Whether the person serving wine is a sommelier or a dining room server, the wine should always be served following this procedure:

1. The wine should be presented to the host at the table so the label can be examined.

2. Once the host has approved the label, the top of the bottle is wiped with a clean cloth.

3. The cork is carefully removed using any type of cork removal tool.

4. The cork is presented to the host for inspection.

5. A small portion is poured into the correct glass for the host to taste. If, for some reason, the wine is unsatisfactory, the server must graciously take the wine back and offer the wine list again.

6. Once the host has tasted and approved the wine, the server pours wine for the rest of the party (see *Exhibit 5f*).

The wineglasses should not be filled to the top, but somewhere between one-half and two-thirds of the way full; this should be a standard that the restaurant has established. The wine is left on the table, perhaps wrapped in a towel, if it is not emptied with the first pouring. If the wine is a chilled white wine, it should be placed in an ice bucket on or near the table. Wine that is visible to diners at other tables helps to merchandise wine, as well as making the wine available to the host to pour more as needed.

Exhibit 5f

Serving wine with elegance involves some ceremony.

Wineglasses

Wineglasses come in many shapes, sizes, and degrees of decoration. Most restaurants use relatively plain wineglasses of only a few basic types: red wine, white wine, sparkling wine, and cordial. (See *Exhibit 5g.*) Prior to serving wine to a table, the waitstaff should set out the proper type of wineglass for each person drinking wine.

Exhibit 5g

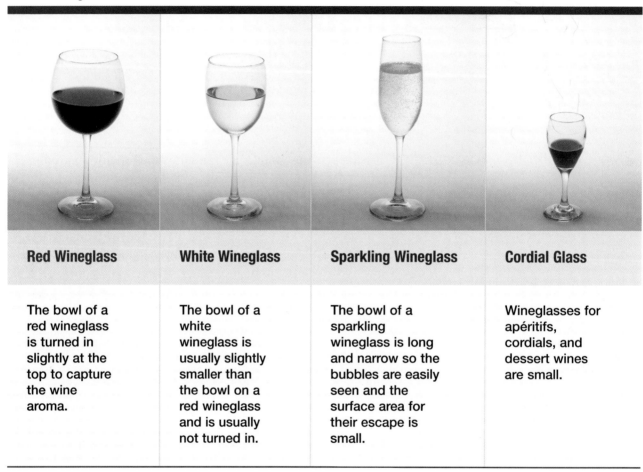

Red Wineglass	White Wineglass	Sparkling Wineglass	Cordial Glass
The bowl of a red wineglass is turned in slightly at the top to capture the wine aroma.	The bowl of a white wineglass is usually slightly smaller than the bowl on a red wineglass and is usually not turned in.	The bowl of a sparkling wineglass is long and narrow so the bubbles are easily seen and the surface area for their escape is small.	Wineglasses for apéritifs, cordials, and dessert wines are small.

Think About It...

What causes you to order a particular mixed drink at a restaurant?

Merchandising Spirits

Distilled spirits are another classification of alcoholic beverages from fermented grains or other plants. They are higher in alcohol content than wine and beer due to having been distilled, and vary from about 40 to 50 percent alcohol. (See *Exhibit 5h.*)

Distillation is a method by which heat is used to extract alcohol from a liquid containing both alcohol and water. The alcohol vaporizes, and then condenses back to a concentrated liquid form as it cools.

The alcohol content of spirits is measured in proof. **Proof** is a number that represents twice the percentag of alcohol content of the

Exhibit 5h

40% ALC./ VOL. (80 PROOF) 1 LITER
LEMON FLAVORED VODKA
PRODUCED AND BOTTLED IN AHUS SWEDEN

Several of the many types of distilled spirits

distilled liquor. For example, an eighty-proof beverage contains 40 percent alcohol. **Spirits** are also known as liquor or hard liquor, and include grain spirits, plant liquors, fruit liquors, liqueurs, and bitters.

- **Grain spirits** include gin, vodka, and whiskey.

- **Plant liquors** include rum and tequila.

- **Brandy** is a distilled spirit made from fruit. Only brandy made from grapes can be identified simply as brandy. Brandy made from other fruit is labeled with the name of the fruit (e.g., peach brandy). Brandy is usually 80 to 84 proof (40 to 42 percent alcohol).

- **Liqueurs** (also known as **cordials**) are made from grain, plant, or fruit spirits, and flavored with herbs, spices, fruits, nuts, or other components. Most are then usually aged to fully develop their flavors. They are sweet and used as after-dinner drinks or as an ingredient in other alcoholic beverages.

- **Bitters**—made with herbs or roots—are used as ingredients in other drinks and have a distinctive flavorful, bitter taste.

Spirits are used as an ingredient in mixed drinks or served alone. To merchandise spirits, a list of the featured brands and house specialty drinks might be prepared. This does not have to be an extensive list, as customers who enjoy mixed drinks will understand that the bar can prepare other drinks. The list of the house specialty drinks can appear on the regular menu if it is short. It can also appear on table tents with complete descriptions and prices of the concoctions. If the theme of the restaurant is such that a variety of specialty mixed drinks add to the image, then a menu that lists just those mixed drinks can be created. As pictured in *Exhibit 5i*, mixed drinks in such a restaurant are often served in very creative, decorative glassware and with unique garnishes.

Exhibit 5i

Add a distinctive touch to your cocktails with special glassware and unique garnishes.

Exhibit 5j

A brandy snifter has a short stem and a large bowl that bends in at the top to capture the brandy aroma.

Some customers will order their liquor by brand name; these are known as **call liquors** or **call brands,** so it is a good idea to find out which brands appeal to your customers. Call brands are usually priced higher than the same type of liquor of a lesser brand—this is true even if the called-for brand is the house brand.

Spirits may be listed on the menu by brand. Because spirits are often aged, the list may include this information as well. For example, a twelve-year-old single malt scotch whiskey may be priced higher than another less distinctive scotch. The spirits list, as with the wine list, should be prepared within the context of the restaurant's image, brand, menu, and customers' expectations.

Brandies and liqueurs are often listed on a dessert menu along with the desserts and special coffees typically ordered at this time. This list could be presented as a separate menu to diners after they have completed their meal, or it could appear on the food menu if only a limited selection is offered. Brandies include Crème de Menthe (mint-flavored brandy), and such fruit-flavored brandies as Benedictine and Cointreau. Liqueurs include, for example, Amaretto, Drambuie, Grand Marnier, and Kahlúa. There are hundreds of liqueurs on the market.

Brandy and liqueurs are better served in appropriate glassware made to highlight their aroma and taste. (See *Exhibit 5j.*) A true brandy lover will appreciate this attention to detail demonstrated by the restaurant.

Exhibit 5k

Beers and ales are available in different flavors and strengths.

Merchandising Beers and Ales

In general, beers are classified as lagers or ales. **Lager** beer is made from bottom-fermenting yeast at cooler temperatures; typically, it is clear, smooth, crisp, golden in color, and slightly bitter. Lager is the more popular type of beer in the United States, and the term is often used synonymously with beer to distinguish it from ale. (See *Exhibit 5k.*) **Ale** is made from top-fermenting yeast at warmer temperatures. Typically, ales are pale and bright in color with a hearty, tart (perhaps bitter) taste. Ales were developed in the British Isles, while lagers are from Germany. Today, many countries throughout the world produce and export beers.

Beer contains 3 to 7 percent alcohol. There are "light" beers sold in the United States, named as such because they contain fewer calories than regular beer. There are also some nonalcohol beers on the market, but they may actually contain up to 0.5 percent alcohol.

Beer is made from water, malt, hops, and yeast. The type of water used is important because of the mineral content it may contain. **Malt** is made from the grain of barley, the sugars of which are fermented in beer production (there are beers made from wheat grains; they are called **wheat beer**). **Hops** are clusters of blossoms from the hop vine and are cared for carefully. The variety of hops, the soil, and the climate provide unique flavoring characteristics that give beers their flavor and aroma. **Yeast** is a living microorganism. It is used to change the sugars in the grains and hops into carbon dioxide and alcohol, and to contribute to flavor.

One of the differences between lager and ale is the way in which they are fermented. The fermentation process of lager beer results in a taste that is mildly bitter, but clean and crisp. Familiar brands of lager include Budweiser, Coors, and Miller. Ales are often served warmer than lagers and have a hearty, robust flavor, with a more pronounced hop or malt taste. Two examples of ales include Bass and Newcastle Brown.

There are several major types of beer and ale:

- **Draft beer** is beer drawn from a tap and propelled by carbonation from a keg.

- **Porter** is a heavier, dark brown, strongly flavored ale produced from malt roasted at high temperatures; it has a slightly higher alcohol content than other ales.

- **Stout** is another member of the ale family and is characterized by a strong, bittersweet flavor; it has an even darker color and a higher alcohol content than porter.

- **Malt liquor** is generally considered a type of beer with a slightly higher alcohol content than other beer, although any beer produced from malt barley can be called a malt beverage. The alcohol content varies from 5 to 8 percent alcohol. Malt liquor has a fruity or spicy flavor.

- **Bock beer** is a traditional German beer that is produced in the autumn and allowed to age until spring—when it is then consumed. It is richer and sweeter in flavor, darker in color, and higher in alcohol content than most lagers.

Beer Menu

Beer may be listed on the regular menu if there are only a few offered. Most customers expect to see two or three draft beers on tap, a handful of domestic beers, and a few imported beers. If the restaurant has a theme that is focused on beer (for example, a microbrewery), then it should feature a more extensive list of beer or a separate beer menu. As with the other categories of alcoholic beverages, however, the restaurant's brand image, type of food served, customers, and costs must be considered when offering beer. A well-chosen, somewhat limited selection of beer is often sufficient to meet the demands of customers.

Pricing Alcoholic Beverages

Alcoholic beverage pricing is often done differently from food pricing. Alcoholic beverage pricing may be even more dependent on what the market will bear than food item pricing. For example, customers do not see a difference between a bottle of a particular brand of domestic beer served in one restaurant, and a bottle of the same brand served in another restaurant. Alcoholic beverage prices are usually marked up more than food items. For example, if a restaurant has targeted a 33 percent food cost (200 percent markup), then it might target a 20 percent beverage cost (400 percent markup).

Exhibit 5l

The prices charged for wine depend on several factors.

Pricing Wine by the Bottle

Wine is usually priced by the bottle, and the gross profit in dollars is used more often as a target rather than a food cost percentage target. An easy way to accomplish wine pricing is to mark up every bottle to 200 percent of cost (100 percent markup). For example, a bottle of wine that costs $18.50 may be marked up to sell for $37.00.

(See *Exhibit 5l.*) This results in $22.00 of gross profit. Some experts recommend that the prices of the bottles of wine should be similar in range to the prices of the menu entrées, with a very limited number of higher priced wines for customers' celebrations and more discriminating customers.

If marking up all the wines to 200 percent of cost results in an average wine bottle cost too far above the average entrée cost, it may be necessary to reduce the markup somewhat or turn to a cheaper wine. If using a 75 percent markup, for example, still produces $10.00 or $12.00 dollars of gross profit, it could be sufficient. It will still increase guest check averages, provide the customer with a wine purchase they might not otherwise make, and contribute significantly to the gross profit margin. To calculate a markup of 75 percent, the cost of the wine is multiplied by 1.75 to determine the bottle price. Consider the following example of a bottle that costs $15.00 and has a markup of 75 percent above cost:

Wine bottle cost × **100% + Markup %** = **Wine bottle price**

$15.00 × 175% = **$26.25**

$15.00 × 1.75 = **$26.25**

$26.25 is the mathematical price of the bottle of wine; the actual menu price would probably be $26.95 or $27. The gross profit is $11.95 on this bottle of wine. If the average entrée price is between $20.00 and $28.00, then the price of the wine is within the entrée range. If the markup had been 100 percent above the cost of the wine, the price would have been 200 percent times the bottle cost, or $30.00. This wine price would have been a little higher than the average entrée price.

Activity

Pricing Wine by the Bottle

Eduardo has been given the responsibility of pricing the wine list. He has been directed to make at least $10.00 in gross profit from each wine. The average entrée cost in this restaurant is between $18.00 and $25.00. He has found the cost of two of the bottles of wine to be $10.00 and $15.00. Determine the markup and menu price for each bottle of wine.

	Bottle 1: $10.00	Bottle 2: $15.00
Markup	_____	_____
Menu price	_____	_____

Pricing Wine by the Glass

Wine is sometimes priced and served by the glass. To establish a price for wine served by the glass, a **standard pour**—the standard number of glasses of wine poured from each bottle—is set. Establishments may set a standard pour of four or five glasses of wine from each bottle. The price for each glass of wine is then determined by dividing the bottle menu price by four or five. A set amount of $1.00 is frequently then added to the amount determined. For example, if a bottle of wine is priced at $25.00 and the standard pour is set at five glasses per bottle, then the price of the glass of wine is $5.00 plus the set amount of $1.00. This glass of wine would be sold for $6.00.

Pricing Spirits

The cost of spirits can be determined by figuring out the number of pours from a bottle. The average mixed drink is made with 1.5 ounces of liquor. A bottle of scotch containing 750 milliliters has 25.4 ounces of liquor. To determine the number of drinks that can be made from this bottle, divide 25.4 ounces by 1.5 ounces per drink. This results in 16.9 drinks.

$$\text{Ounces per bottle} \div \text{Ounces per drink} = \text{Number of drinks per bottle}$$

$$25.4 \text{ oz} \div 1.5 \text{ oz} = 16.9 \text{ drinks}$$

However, one problem with pouring liquor is that some portion is inevitably lost through pouring mistakes, evaporation, or spillage. A bartender can make drinks using the free-pour method in which one hand holds the spirits bottle and the other pours the mixer. A problem with this method is that it is relatively easy to overpour or underpour the 1.5 ounces. A second method is using a jigger or shot glass to measure the liquor. This method is more accurate, but slows down the process of making drinks. There are control devices that can be attached to the bottles of liquor to deliver precise measurements, but they must be clean to work correctly. There also are mechanical dispensers that deliver accurate amounts of alcoholic beverages, but they are expensive and rarely used.

Because of the difficulties in producing the exact amount of liquor with every pour, a **set loss** figure is established for each bottle. This figure is frequently 5 percent or so. For a 750 milliliter (25.4 ounce) bottle, a 5 percent set loss is 1.27 ounces.

Set loss percentage $\times$ **Ounces per bottle** $=$ **Set loss per bottle**

5% $\times$ 25.4 oz $=$ 1.27 oz

.05 $\times$ 25.40 oz $=$ 1.27 oz

Therefore, the 25.4 ounces of liquor from the scotch bottle becomes much closer to twenty-four ounces.

Ounces per bottle $-$ Set loss $=$ Salable liquor per bottle

25.4 oz $-$ 1.27 oz $=$ 24.13 oz

Therefore, the actual number of pours from this bottle is sixteen.

Ounces per bottle $\div$ Ounces per drink $=$ Number of pours per bottle

24.13 oz $\div$ 1.5 oz $=$ 16.08 pours

Once the number of pours has been determined, the price of the bottle is divided by the pours per bottle (in this example, sixteen) to get the cost of the liquor in each drink. If the 750 milliliter bottle cost is $20.00, then the cost of the liquor used in each pour is $1.25.

Cost of bottle $\div$ Pours per bottle $=$ Liquor cost per drink

$20.00 $\div$ 16 $=$ $1.25

The food cost of mixed drinks also includes the cost of the other ingredients in the drink. These can be determined individually for each kind of drink, or—more realistically—handled as an average cost for mixers, garnishes, etc. This average cost could be a dollar amount, such as $0.25 per drink, or it could be a percentage added in relation to the cost of the liquor, such as 20 or 25 percent of the cost of the liquor. If the cost of a drink made with scotch is $1.25 for the scotch and $0.25 for the other ingredients, the total food cost of the drink is $1.50.

To determine the menu price for the drink, divide the target food cost percentage into the actual food cost for the drink. Since the target food cost percentage for spirits is 20 or 25 percent of the food cost, the price can be determined by dividing the food cost of the drink by 20 or 25 percent.

$$\text{Food cost} \ \div \ \text{Target food cost percentage} \ = \ \text{Calculated menu price}$$

$$\$1.50 \div 20\% = \$7.50$$

$$\$1.50 \div .20 = \$7.50$$

If the target food cost percentage is established at 25 percent, then the resulting alcoholic beverage price is $6.00.

Other foodservice operations determine an average cost of drinks and set them all at the same price based on a fairly high markup, such as 400 percent (20 percent food cost). As with menu pricing, the prices are based on the brand image of the restaurant, the competitive market, the amount customers are willing to pay, and pricing psychology.

Pricing Beer and Ale

The prices for beer are determined in two ways, depending on how the beer or ale is sold.

- If the beer is sold by the bottle, the price is usually established using a markup method with a target 20 or 25 percent cost, much like the mixed drinks made from spirits.

- If the beer is draft beer sold by the glass, then the cost of the beer is determined from the number of drinks that can be poured from a barrel. As with spirits, there is a pour loss associated with draft beer; this is usually 7 to 8 percent. Therefore, the loss has to be considered when establishing the actual number of glasses of beer that can be served from the barrel. The cost of the glass of beer is based on the actual number of pours, considering loss, in exactly the same way as the cost of spirits. The actual cost is then marked up based on the target cost of 20 to 25 percent.

Always remember that the amount the customer is willing to pay for beer has a large impact on what the price will be, as does the market, the brand image, and pricing psychology.

Activity

Pricing Spirits by the Drink

Eduardo has done well on pricing wine, so now he has been given the responsibility of pricing the mixed and straight spirit drinks. His bar specializes in oversized drinks with 2.0 ounces of liquor in each drink. In addition, the bar buys large 1.75 liter bottles for $30.00 each to save money. These bottles are harder to handle, so the set loss is 5.5 percent. On the oversized drinks, the mixer and garnish add 25 percent to the cost of the alcohol. If the bar works at a 25 percent target food cost percentage, what should be the menu price for these drinks? Go through the following series of calculations to determine this.

1. What is the set loss amount per bottle?_____

2. How much salable liquor is in a bottle?_____

3. How many pours are there in a bottle?_____

4. What is the liquor cost per drink? _____

5. What is the cost of the other ingredients per drink?_____

6. What is the total food cost per drink?_____

7. What should be the menu price for these drinks?_____

Summary

Offering alcoholic beverages to the customer is an important part of many restaurants' operations. It is also important to observe the state and local laws applying to the sale and service of alcoholic beverages. Ways to present the liquor menu to the guest include offering the beer, wine, and spirits on the food menu, or on separate menus if the lists are extensive. Dessert menus may include desserts, after-dinner drinks, such as brandies and liqueurs, and specialty coffees. Methods for listing wines and spirits include indicating the distinctive features of each, such as brand name or vintner, year of harvest or production, descriptions of the wine or drinks made from the spirits, and suggestions of food items that would be enhanced by a particular wine. Wines include table wines, fortified wines, sparkling wines, apéritifs, and dessert wines. Distilled spirits include grain spirits, plant liquors, fruit liquors, liqueurs, and bitters. In the United States, liqueurs and cordials are interchangeable terms. Beer includes lagers and ales. Lagers make up the majority of familiar beer in the United States. Ways to price alcoholic beverages include gross profit targets on larger quantities like bottles and markup pricing for glasses and mixed drinks.

Review Your Learning

1 What is the alcohol content of a spirit labeled as 80 proof?

A. 160% C. 40%

B. 80% D. 20%

2 How are fortified wines made?

A. Top-fermenting yeast at cool temperatures

B. Bottom-fermenting yeast at warmer temperatures

C. Adding carbon dioxide to the bottle during fermentation

D. Adding brandy to wine during fermentation

3 The most important fruit liquors are

A. brandies. C. crèmes.

B. liqueurs. D. apértifis.

4 Pricing wine by the bottle

A. often results in a price far out of range of the entrées.

B. is often based on a 20 percent food cost.

C. generally includes an extra charge of $1.00 per bottle.

D. often uses a gross profit measured in dollars.

5 Sparkling wines have an alcohol content of

A. 40–50% C. 13–14%

B. 16–24% D. 3–7%

6 What information should wine lists include?

A. The wines available on tap and in bottles

B. All the wines, listed alphabetically by vintner

C. Type of wine, vintner, and year

D. Domestic wines and foreign wines in separate categories

7 Lager beer includes

A. stout and porter.

B. top-fermented beer.

C. beer made from wheat grains.

D. bottom-fermented beer.

8 What information should be included on beer menus?

A. Type of beer, brewery, region, and year

B. Tap and bottled beers in separate categories

C. Local beers and national brands in separate categories

D. High-profit beers first, then other beers

9 Pour loss should be considered when

A. determining the number of drinks from a bottle or keg.

B. determining how many bottles of wine there are in a case.

C. providing your customer with a bottle of beer.

D. determining how many brandies to put on the menu.

10 Although alcoholic beverages can contribute strongly to profits, they can also result in additional expenses because

A. liquor laws must be strictly followed.

B. spoilage is a constant cause of lost profits.

C. spillage causes a lot of waste and lost profits.

D. employees give away too many drinks to friends.

Menu Item Sales Performance Analysis

6

After completing this chapter, you should be able to:

- Analyze menu item sales performance.

- Calculate sales volume percentage and sales dollar percentage.

- Define profitability and target contribution margins.

- Analyze and evaluate the menu using item counts, subjective evaluation, popularity indexes, contribution margin, and day-part information.

Test Your Knowledge

1. **True or False:** "Day part" refers to the time of day everyone comes to work. *(See p. 118.)*

2. **True or False:** Gross profit is the amount of money remaining after all expenses have been paid. *(See p. 113.)*

3. **True or False:** Item counts are one of several daily tasks that must be done by hand. *(See p. 116.)*

4. **True or False:** A popularity factor can assist in the evaluation of menu items found in competing categories. *(See p. 110.)*

5. **True or False:** Subjective evaluation of menu items is based on opinion. *(See p. 117.)*

Key Terms

80-20 rule	Item count	Sales dollar percentage
Contribution margin	Margin	Sales volume
Day part	Pareto principle	Sales volume percentage
Day-part analysis	Popularity factor	Subjective evaluation
Expected popularity	Popularity index	Target margin
Gross profit	Profitability	

Introduction

Once a menu has been researched, its items selected, its prices determined, and its layout designed, a performance analysis is needed to determine the success of the menu's offerings. Most types of evaluations depend on sales and other operational information. Profitability measures should also be calculated. Determining item counts, contribution margins, popularity indexes, and day-part contributions can all be useful in evaluating a menu.

Some experts say that an evaluation of menu items should be conducted at least four times each year, or when experiencing a major change in sales or profits.

This chapter will help you analyze menus from a variety of perspectives. It is important to understand how each menu item fares in relation to other menu items in terms of sales, profitability, contribution margin, and time of day. Being able to calculate this information will help you make decisions regarding individual menu items.

Sales Evaluation Measures

The sales performance of each menu item can be determined after the restaurant has been open for some time and sales data can be analyzed. Gathering information for three months or longer provides more useful results than data from a shorter time period.

Reviewing sales volume numbers for the day can help evaluate a menu item.

Evaluating by Sales Volume Percentage

The sales volume of a menu item is the number of times the item is sold in a time period: a day, a week, or a month, although a short time period can be misleading. Generally, this information is sorted by category, such as appetizers, entrées, and so forth. The quantity of each menu item sold can be recorded by hand or by many of the point-of-sale (POS) systems now used in restaurants. (See *Exhibit 6a.*) The result would be a table of sales data much like the first two columns of *Exhibit 6b.*

Sales volume information can be further used to compare the number of each menu item sold to the total number of menu items sold in the same time period; or, in other words, each menu item's sales can be expressed as a percentage of total sales. This is called the sales volume percentage.

$$\left(\begin{array}{c} \text{Item sales} \\ \text{volume} \end{array} \div \begin{array}{c} \text{Sales volume} \\ \text{of all items} \end{array} \right) \times 100 = \begin{array}{c} \text{Sales volume} \\ \text{percentage} \end{array}$$

The sales performance of some menu items is shown in *Exhibit 6b* in the *Sales Volume %* column. This column indicates that the Rib Eye Steak sells the most by volume, almost 28 percent of total sales, while the Planked Salmon sells the least, only 12.5 percent of total sales.

Exhibit 6b

Sales-Related Evaluation Measures

Entrée	Sales Volume	Sales Volume %	Menu Price	Item Sales	Sales Dollar %
Skewered Shrimp with Fried Rice	37	24.3%	$12.95	$ 479.15	22.0%
Pork Medallions with Sweet Potato	25	16.5	15.50	387.50	17.8
Rib Eye Steak with Onion Rings	42	27.6	14.95	627.90	28.9
Herbed Chicken with Stuffing	29	19.1	12.95	375.55	17.3
Planked Salmon with Asparagus	19	12.5	15.95	303.05	14.0
Total	152	100.0%		$2,173.15	100.0%

Evaluation by Sales Dollar Percentage

Determining the sales dollar percentage for each menu item is also useful for menu evaluation purposes. The **sales dollar percentage** is the percentage of sales a menu item accounts for, expressed in dollars rather than volume. In this calculation, (see *Exhibit 6b* on p. 105) the sales dollar amount of each menu item is determined as before, by multiplying the quantity sold of each menu item (*Sales Volume* column) by its menu price, (*Menu Price* column). Then the percentage of sales each menu item contributes to total sales can be found by dividing each item's sales dollars (*Item Sales* column) by the total sales dollars for all items.

$$\left(\begin{array}{c} \textbf{Item sales} \\ \textbf{dollars} \end{array} \div \begin{array}{c} \textbf{Total sales} \\ \textbf{dollars} \end{array} \right) \times\ \textbf{100}\ =\ \begin{array}{c} \textbf{Sales dollar} \\ \textbf{percentage} \end{array}$$

The results of these calculations for our example are found in *Exhibit 6b* on p. 105, in the *Sales Dollar %* column.

Activity

Calculating Sales Dollar Percentage

Sally, the assistant manager of a restaurant, has been asked to do a menu analysis. The manager thinks that there are too many entrées on the luncheon menu and is concerned about the sales percentage of each item. The manager would like to remove at least one item from the luncheon menu in order to streamline kitchen operations. Sally has been given the information shown in the table below, gathered from yesterday's records.

Determine the sales dollar percentage of each item. Then decide which item to remove from the menu based on its sales dollar percentage.

Entrée	Number Sold	Menu Price	Total Sales Dollars	Sales Dollar %
Fish and Chips	42	$9.95		
Giant Hamburger	51	8.50		
Reuben Sandwich	25	7.75		
House Club Sandwich	27	5.75		
Crab Salad in Pita	21	7.95		
Vegetarian Wrap with Cheese	23	6.95		
TOTAL	**189**			

Which one should be removed? _____

Popularity Evaluation Measures

Popularity measures build upon sales-related measures in ways that are more useful and easier to understand. These measures include:

■ Popularity index

■ Popularity factor

Popularity Index

One evaluation tool that can be used is the popularity index. A **popularity index** is a way to measure the popularity of a specific menu item in relation to other menu items in its category. A popularity index can also be used to measure the popularity of a particular category of menu items against competing categories of menu items. Popularity indexes are best calculated using sales records for several weeks, rather than just for a day. They are important in observing popularity trends for menu items.

Calculating the Popularity Index

A popularity index is essentially the sales volume percentage for a menu item within its menu category. To determine the popularity index, the number of each item sold in a category is divided by the total number of items sold in the category.

$$\left(\begin{array}{c} \textbf{Item sales} \\ \textbf{volume} \end{array} \div \begin{array}{c} \textbf{Sales volume of} \\ \textbf{all category items} \end{array} \right) \times \textbf{100} = \begin{array}{c} \textbf{Popularity} \\ \textbf{index} \end{array}$$

To continue with the example (see *Exhibit 6b* on page 105), 37 Skewered Shrimp entrées and 25 Pork Medallion entrées were sold. These entrées came from a list of five, and the total sales count for all entrées was 152. To determine the popularity index for the Skewered Shrimp entrée, the count of 37 sold is divided by the total entrée count of 152 to get a popularity index of 24.3. To determine the popularity index for the Pork Medallions entrée, the count of 25 sold is divided by 152 to get a popularity index of 16.5. (*Note:* these numbers are the same as the sales volume percentage numbers shown in *Exhibit 6b* on p. 105 because the sales volume percentage example was for a single menu category.)

Evaluating the Popularity Index

Popularity indexes should be used with caution for several reasons:

■ Sales from different days of the week may be different. For example, customers who arrive on weekends may generate more sales of a particular menu item than customers during the week.

- If a popularity index is compared to other factors, such as menu prices, it might become apparent that customers are purchasing lower-priced menu items.

- Some low-popularity menu items may be purchased by a sufficient number of customers so that it would be unwise to remove those items from the menu, especially if those items are measured using other methods, such as their contribution margin or their subjective evaluation scores (discussed later in this chapter).

Additionally, unusual occurrences can affect which menu items are selected and in what quantities. As a consequence, the popularity index would be misleading. For example:

- Serving the same menu item to a luncheon party of sixty would certainly impact the popularity index for that day or even that week.

- If a menu item sold out during a certain time of day, this would limit the number that could have been sold, thereby skewing the item count for that meal service.

- The quality of a product served during a particular time period could result in skewed counts of sales.

- A piece of kitchen equipment that was not working may have forced the removal of one or several items from availability.

Often, restaurants will maintain the manager's comments about unusual events that happened. (See *Exhibit 6c.*) These comments should be reviewed when evaluating the popularity index so that anything that might affect menu item sales can be included in the evaluation.

Exhibit 6c

Manager's Comments

	NOTES
May 8	Party of 60 at lunch; pre-ordered the rib eye steak for everyone.
May 13	Ran out of Skewered Shrimp halfway through dinner.
June 1	Kitchen fire caused early closing at 7:00p.m.
June 16	Bad shipment of chicken; pulled herbed chicken from menu

A manager's notes provide information that can explain menu item sales.

Comparing Menu Items

To evaluate the popularity index of items within a category, simply compare the numbers. The higher the popularity index, the more popular the item.

There are several ways to evaluate the performance of items in one category against items in a competing category. In all cases, item counts are collected for each of the two categories. The simplest way to compare items from different categories is to simply compare their popularity indexes. For example, a salad with a popularity index of 0.18 looks better than a sandwich with a popularity index of 0.17.

However, this simple comparison can be misleading if the two categories contain different numbers of items. The remaining comparison methods take care of this situation.

Exhibit 6d

Expected Popularity

Entrée	Expected Popularity
Skewered Shrimp with Fried Rice	0.18
Pork Medallions with Sweet Potato	0.12
Rib Eye Steak with Onion Rings	0.32
Herbed Chicken with Stuffing	0.23
Planked Salmon with Asparagus	0.15
Total	**1.00**

Expected Popularity

The **expected popularity** for a specific item in a group of menu items is the popularity that the item is expected to have by some authority. For example, management might expect that some entrées would be more popular than others, as shown in *Exhibit 6d*.

In the absence of specific expectations of popularity, you should expect all the items of a group to be equally popular. If this is the case, then the total popularity must be divided equally among the items, as expressed in the following formula:

$$1 \div \frac{\text{Number of elements in group}}{} = \frac{\text{Expected equal popularity}}{}$$

For example, if a group contains five items, then each would have an expected popularity of one-fifth, or 20 percent. If a group contains ten items, then each would have an expected popularity of one-tenth, or 10 percent.

If the salad category includes five entrée salads and the sandwich category includes six sandwiches, then the popularity indexes of items in these categories cannot be evaluated directly against each other.

Instead, you must compare each item's popularity index against the item's expected popularity. The expected equal popularity of each of the five entrée salads is 0.20, and the expected equal popularity of each of the six sandwiches is 0.167. Thus, it would appear that the salad with a popularity of 0.18 is performing below expectations, while the sandwich with a popularity of 0.17 is performing slightly above expectations. (See *Exhibit 6e.*)

Exhibit 6e

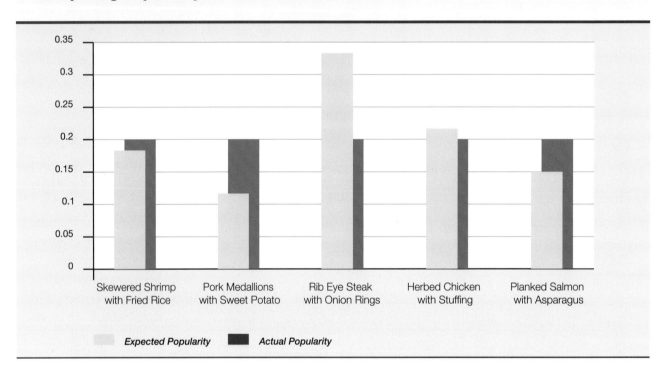

Comparing Popularity Indexes of Menu Items

Popularity Factor

To make comparisons between competing categories of menu items less difficult, it is useful to develop a popularity factor. A **popularity factor** is calculated by dividing the popularity index of each menu item in a category by its expected popularity.

| **Item's popularity index** | ÷ | **Item's expected popularity** | = | **Popularity factor** |

There are three possible situations that account for the popularity factor of a menu item in comparison to its expected popularity, resulting in three distinct value ranges for an item's popularity factor:

1 If a menu item is performing as expected, the numerator and denominator are the same, and the item's popularity factor is 1.00.

2 If an item is performing better than expected, the item's popularity index (the numerator) is greater than the item's expected popularity (the denominator), and the popularity factor is greater than 1.00.

3 If an item is performing worse than expected, the item's popularity index (the numerator) is smaller than the item's expected popularity (the denominator), and the popularity factor is less than 1.00.

For example, an entrée salad has an actual popularity index of 0.18 and an expected popularity of 0.20. The popularity factor calculation results in 0.90.

0.18 ÷ 0.20 = 0.90

The entrée salad is not selling as well as expected.

In another example, a sandwich has an actual popularity index of 0.17 and an expected popularity of 0.167. The popularity factor calculation results in 1.02.

0.17 ÷ 0.167 = 1.02

The sandwich is performing slightly better than expected.

Exhibit 6f

An efficient kitchen staff is critical to the success of a menu item.

Once the popularity factors for menu items have been determined, decisions can be made about whether to remove an item from a menu, or market it differently. As with all decisions about menu items, consideration should be given to kitchen efficiencies (see *Exhibit 6f*), actual costs of producing the items, their contributions to total sales, the restaurant's brand image, customers' expectations, and other factors taking place when the items were sold (such as, which meal period, which day of the week, or what the weather was like).

Activity

Calculating Popularity Index and Popularity Factor

Sally has been asked to evaluate the menu items in the salad and sandwich categories of the menu so that her manager can determine which item to remove.

1️⃣ Complete the Popularity Index column in the table below.

2️⃣ Identify the item with the lowest popularity across both categories.

_____

_____

Sally's manager wants to see how each menu item is doing in comparison to its expected popularity before deciding what to remove from these menu categories.

3️⃣ Calculate the popularity factor for each menu item.

4️⃣ Recommend which item to remove from each category on its popularity factor.

_____

_____

Popularity for Different Categories				
Menu Item	**Expected Popularity**	**Actual Sales**	**Popularity Index**	**Popularity Factor**
Sandwich Category				
Bacon, Lettuce, and Tomato	0.167	52		
Turkey Club	0.167	23		
Monté Cristo	0.167	37		
Tuna Melt	0.167	86		
Reuben	0.167	21		
California Chicken Wrap	0.167	67		
Sandwich Total	**1.000**	**286**		
Salad Category				
Oriental Chicken	0.200	18		
Cobb	0.200	32		
Taco	0.200	41		
Cajun Shrimp	0.200	16		
Wilted Spinach with Bacon	0.200	21		
Salad Total	**1.000**	**128**		

Profitability Evaluation Measures

Profitability has been defined as the excess of revenue over expenses in a series of transactions. Profitability in restaurant operations is the comparison of revenue from the sale of menu items with the cost of the food or beverages used to prepare them. This difference is also called the **margin;** most restaurants set a **target margin** for their operation, which is a goal amount.

Item Contribution Margin

Profitability is based on the **contribution margin** or **gross profit**—the amount of money remaining after the cost of goods sold (for example, food and beverages) is subtracted from pretax revenues.

$$\begin{matrix} \textbf{Total} \\ \textbf{revenue} \end{matrix} - \begin{matrix} \textbf{Total cost of} \\ \textbf{goods sold} \end{matrix} = \begin{matrix} \textbf{Contribution} \\ \textbf{margin} \end{matrix} \ or \ \begin{matrix} \textbf{Gross} \\ \textbf{profit} \end{matrix}$$

Menu items are often evaluated based on their individual gross profitability, and therefore, their contributions to the total profitability of an operation. To make this determination, the food cost attributed to the preparation of each menu item must be known, as well as the menu selling price. Then the food cost of the menu item is subtracted from the menu selling price. The remainder is the item's gross profit or contribution margin.

$$\begin{matrix} \textbf{Item selling} \\ \textbf{price} \end{matrix} - \begin{matrix} \textbf{Item food} \\ \textbf{cost} \end{matrix} = \begin{matrix} \textbf{Item contribution} \\ \textbf{margin} \end{matrix} \ or \ \begin{matrix} \textbf{Item gross} \\ \textbf{profit} \end{matrix}$$

Exhibit 6g shows the gross profits for the sample menu items.

In examining the gross profit generated by each item, it can be seen that each sale of the Planked Salmon contributes the most to the gross profit, while each sale of the Skewered Shrimp contributes the least.

Exhibit 6g

Menu Item Gross Profits

Entrée	Menu Price	Food Cost	Item Gross Profit
Skewered Shrimp with Fried Rice	$12.95	$4.51	$ 8.44
Pork Medallions with Sweet Potato	15.50	5.71	9.79
Rib Eye Steak with Onion Rings	14.95	5.38	9.57
Herbed Chicken with Stuffing	12.95	3.37	9.58
Planked Salmon with Asparagus	15.95	5.90	10.05

Total Contribution Margin

The total contribution margin for an item is determined by multiplying the contribution margin for each menu item by the number sold for that item.

Item contribution margin	×	Number of items sold	=	Total contribution margin

The information gained from these calculations will provide a picture of the items that are contributing the most to profit and to the payment of expenses. The total contribution margins for our example are shown in *Exhibit 6h*.

Exhibit 6h

Total Contribution Margins

Entrée	Gross Profit	Number Sold	Total Contribution Margin
Skewered Shrimp with Fried Rice	$ 8.44	37	$312.28
Pork Medallions with Sweet Potato	9.79	25	244.75
Rib Eye Steak with Onion Rings	9.57	42	401.94
Herbed Chicken with Stuffing	9.58	29	277.82
Planked Salmon with Asparagus	10.05	19	190.95

The Rib Eye Steak contributes the most money to gross profit when sales volume is considered. When examining the gross profit of the menu items earlier, it looked as though the Planked Salmon contributed the most to gross profit and the Skewered Shrimp the least. Now, it appears that the Skewered Shrimp contributes the second-highest amount to gross profit based on its sales. The analysis of the total contribution for each item changes the apparent profitability of the menu items. Had a decision been made earlier based on gross profit, the Skewered Shrimp would have been taken off the menu, and the item that contributes the second-most money overall would no longer be sold. This analysis illustrates why menu items need to be analyzed using more than one method, or a combination of methods, in order to make sound decisions.

Evaluating Menu Items

Evaluation of menu items requires the menu evaluator to compare and contrast all the available information:

- Sales volume

- Popularity index

- Popularity factor

- Item gross profit (contribution margin)

The various items do not always agree. For example, the Rib Eye Steak is the highest-selling item in terms of sales volume. It contributes the largest percentage of sales to the total sales volume, but it is fourth in item contribution margin. The Skewered Shrimp is the second highest-selling item in sales volume, second in percentage of total sales, but last in item contribution margin. The Pork Medallions are fourth in sales volume and third in sales percentage, but second in item contribution margin.

Decisions about menu items have to be made with several factors in mind, not just sales, popularity, or margin factors. If you look only at these factors, an incorrect decision could be made. For example, you must take into account preparation costs, service costs, and the image of the establishment. When you do this, things get more complicated. For example:

- The Planked Salmon has the largest contribution margin. However, if it is the most labor-intensive to prepare, a lot of its contribution margin could be used up by labor costs.

- The menu items should accurately reflect your brand image and meet customers' expectations.

- If no one is sure what "planked" salmon is, then that might explain why it is the lowest-selling entrée. That problem could be fixed by adding a menu description.

- The Planked Salmon is also the highest-priced menu item, while the Herbed Chicken and Skewered Shrimp have the lowest menu prices. And although the Rib Eye Steak has a higher menu price, it outsells both the chicken and shrimp entrées. Therefore, customers are not merely ordering based on the lowest price.

If the decision of which item to remove from the menu is based on contribution margin, then the Skewered Shrimp must be removed. If the decision of which item to remove from the menu is based on lowest sales volume, then the Planked Salmon must be removed. You must also consider the effect that the preparation of a menu item has on the efficiency of the kitchen, whether or not an item supports the brand image, and most important, the customers' expectations.

Activity

Calculating Item and Total Contribution Margins

Sally's manager wants to consider each menu item's contribution to gross profit before making any decisions about which item to remove. Calculate this value for each menu item in the chart below and then make your recommendation about which one to remove based on the results.

Menu Item	Actual Sales	Menu Price	Food Cost	Item Contribution Margin	Total Contribution Margin
Sandwich Category					
Bacon, Lettuce, and Tomato	52	$5.50	$2.03		
Turkey Club	23	5.95	1.98		
Monté Cristo	37	7.50	2.20		
Tuna Melt	86	6.50	1.75		
Reuben	21	6.99	2.75		
California Chicken Wrap	67	7.50	2.63		
Sandwich Total	**286**				
Salad Category					
Oriental Chicken	18	$7.50	$2.32		
Cobb	32	6.99	2.47		
Taco	41	6.50	1.73		
Cajun Shrimp	16	7.99	3.10		
Wilted Spinach with Bacon	21	6.50	2.05		
Salad Total	**128**				

Which item would you remove from the menu based on your calculations?

_____

Other Measures Used to Evaluate Menus

There are a variety of other measures used to evaluate menus. One of the evaluation tools includes item counts. **Item count** is the number of items in a list. Item counts can be done for the entire list of items found on a menu. Item counts can also be done for the number of items in each category appearing on the menu. The third way item counts can be used is to count the number of menu items sold, either in a category or for the entire menu. In the previous section, for example, the total number of entrée menu items sold was determined.

The Pareto Principle

Menu expert Banger Smith, of the organization Menus for Profit, says that, regardless of the number of menu items in a category like appetizers or entrées, the top two or three sellers account for a large majority of the sales in that category. If an item count reveals that there are ten or more appetizers on a menu, further analysis is warranted of the number of appetizers sold. It is often found that two or three of the appetizers account for 80 percent or more of appetizer sales. This is in accordance with the **Pareto principle,** also known as the **80-20 rule.** The Pareto principle was named after the Italian economist Vilfredo Pareto, who noted in 1906 that 80 percent of the wealth was owned by 20 percent of the population.

The determination that needs to be made is whether limiting the appetizer list to the most popular items will hurt sales or customers' expectations. It would be appropriate to eliminate the poor sellers if it would:

- Result in more efficient kitchen operations

- Reduce inventory and food costs

- Not affect customers' demands

In many cases, removing the two or three least popular appetizers will not reduce the total sales of appetizers because the remaining items account for a large portion of total sales, and customers will continue to select them.

The item counts (in this case, the number of items on the menu) may reveal that the menu has been growing over time, with little regard to the effect that this growth has on the kitchen dynamic. If the item count for the total number of menu items is large, but the number of items sold for individual menu items is very low for some items, it might be useful to consider their removal from the menu.

Subjective Evaluation

Subjective evaluation, by definition, is an assessment based primarily on opinion. Subjective evaluation of the menu can take two forms; the first one is useful before the restaurant opening, while the second is useful after customers' opinions have been gathered.

In the first form of subjective evaluation, a trained and experienced person looks at the menu and makes a subjective judgment of the effectiveness of the menu. Such menu evaluation experts often use a form that includes many characteristics reviewed in this guide.

Think About It...

What do you do when you are given a restaurant survey to complete? How will you approach it in the future?

Exhibit 6i

Your customer's opinion on menu items is invaluable.

The menu is studied for the following:

- Effectiveness of layout and design principles
- Support for the brand image
- Clarity and accuracy of descriptions
- Menu text's ability to sell items
- Variety in preparation techniques
- Kinds of food offered

The evaluator may also look at the kitchen to determine if the kitchen design, storage areas, and equipment are able to produce the menu items listed. The above evaluations, while admittedly subjective, are based on expert understanding of menus and their execution.

The second form of subjective evaluation is based on customers' opinions of the menu items once the restaurant is open. Customers are surveyed to identify why a particular menu item was chosen over another, or whether their expectations were met. (See *Exhibit 6i* for example.) For example, they may be asked to complete a survey that includes evaluation of the menu items' taste, presentation, variety, price-value relationship, or cost. The restaurant manager should examine the results of these surveys to determine which menu items are favored and which are disliked by customers. If other evaluation measures are considered along with these survey results, useful decisions about menu item changes can be made.

Day-Part Sales

Another useful analysis is to examine day-part sales. A **day part** is the period of the day that a particular meal or menu is served—breakfast, lunch, dinner, afternoon tea, late night, and so forth. A **day-part analysis** determines which items are sold at certain times of the day. In this type of analysis, the sales for each meal period (or service period that uses the same menu or items) is examined, rather than the sales totals for the whole day. The same techniques described earlier in this chapter can be used, based on the sales per day part rather than the sales for the whole day.

For example, if the same menu is used for lunch and dinner, then sales of the menu items at lunch should be counted separately from the sales of the same items at dinner. The sales volume for each menu item can be done for each meal period, and the sales percentage can be figured out separately for each meal period. The gross profit and the total contributions to gross profit can also be calculated by meal, rather than daily.

Think About It...

Have you ever seen a menu designed for a particular time of day (for example, an after-theater menu with desserts and specialty coffees only, or an early-bird dinner menu with just a few of the regular entrées)? Why do you think these types of menus exist?

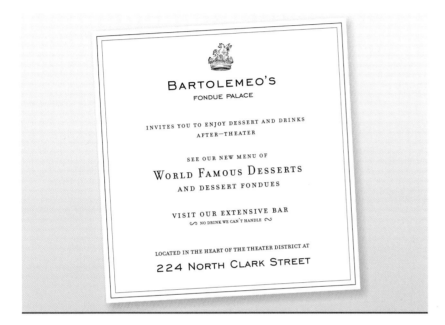

BARTOLEMEO'S
FONDUE PALACE

INVITES YOU TO ENJOY DESSERT AND DRINKS
AFTER—THEATER

SEE OUR NEW MENU OF
WORLD FAMOUS DESSERTS
AND DESSERT FONDUES

VISIT OUR EXTENSIVE BAR
∽ NO DRINK WE CAN'T HANDLE ∽

LOCATED IN THE HEART OF THE THEATER DISTRICT AT
224 NORTH CLARK STREET

Decisions based on the results of this type of analysis may be different from decisions made based on the whole day. Therefore, there may be changes in the menu in which certain items are offered only at lunch and others only at dinner.

Some menus indicate items that are only offered after 4 p.m. or only until 11 a.m., for example. The decision to limit availability is a difficult one to make in attempting to meet customers' expectations. However, these decisions may be based on the information gathered from a day-part analysis of menu item sales, or from the impact the production of these items may have on the kitchen.

Summary

A menu planner spends a lot of time developing a restaurant menu. Market research is done, the brand image is created, the menu items are selected and priced, the kitchen and storage areas are examined, and the menu layout is designed. This chapter has provided some tools to use in analyzing the performance of individual menu items in terms of customer satisfaction and profitability. The sales volume, or popularity index, indicates which items are the most popular and sell the most. The item contribution margin, or gross profit, indicates each item's individual profitability. Total contribution margin takes both of these factors into account to give a broader picture of each item's contribution to the foodservice operation's success. The above calculated figures can be calculated for the whole day, but are more accurate when done for separate day parts. Other considerations include item counts and the effect of stressing the 20 percent of items that generate 80 percent of revenue. But only taking into account these financial figures for menu items ignores other critical factors such as meeting the needs of customers, reinforcing the brand image, and maintaining kitchen efficiency. All these factors must be considered to make sound decisions about menu changes.

Review Your Learning

1 Menu item sales performance analysis is best done with

A. subjective measures only.

B. three months of sales records.

C. your favorite sales analysis tool.

D. item counts for entrées only.

2 The sales percentage for each menu item is found by

A. subtracting the menu item food cost from the menu-selling price.

B. dividing the expected popularity by the actual popularity.

C. dividing the sales of each menu item by the total sales.

D. multiplying the number sold by the gross profit.

3 Subjective evaluation of the menu is often done

A. after the restaurant is open, by the manager.

B. before the restaurant is open, by a trained evaluator.

C. before the restaurant is open, by the chef and the dishwasher.

D. after the restaurant is open, by the dining room hostess.

4 The popularity index is found by

A. counting all the menu items sold in a category and dividing by the total number of menu items sold.

B. dividing the expected popularity of each menu item by its actual popularity.

C. multiplying the contribution margin for each menu item by the number of the items that were sold.

D. asking guests to complete a survey that asks how well they like the menu items.

5 The popularity factor makes it easier to

A. determine the menu items with the highest total contribution margin.

B. evaluate the success of each menu item based on customer survey results.

C. achieve the highest sales based on comments from the servers.

D. make comparisons between competing categories of menu items.

6 Which of the following is *not* a way that menus can be evaluated using item counts?

A. Taking item counts of the entire number of items on the menu

B. Measuring the gross profit of the menu item counts

C. Determining the number of menu items in each category

D. Finding the number of menu items sold in a category

7 It is often found that if there are a large number of menu items in a category,

A. they sell equally well.

B. the customers like 80 percent of them.

C. two or three items account for 80 percent of sales.

D. the kitchen can produce only 80 percent of them quickly.

8 Using several sales analysis tools together

A. gives a better picture of the success of the menu items.

B. is a waste of the manager's time.

C. requires that customers make the most important decisions.

D. ensures that sales volume will not be affected.

Menu Sales Mix Analysis

7

After completing this chapter, you should be able to:

- Perform a menu sales mix analysis.
- Describe other purposes for a menu sales mix analysis.
- Determine menu items' popularity.
- Determine menu items' profitability.
- Classify menu items as stars, plow horses, puzzles, or dogs.
- Change the menu based on the results of the menu sales mix analysis.

Test Your Knowledge

1. **True or False:** A menu sales mix analysis will have little impact on staffing requirements. *(See p. 124.)*

2. **True or False:** A menu sales mix analysis will help determine the most popular items on the menu. *(See p. 123.)*

3. **True or False:** A menu sales mix analysis might suggest moving a menu item's placement on the physical menu. *(See p. 139.)*

4. **True or False:** A menu sales mix analysis will tell you to remove all the unpopular and unprofitable items from the menu. *(See p. 140.)*

5. **True or False:** A menu sales mix analysis needs to be done only once after the restaurant is open. *(See p. 123.)*

Key Terms

Average contribution margin

Cost-margin analysis

Dog

Gross profit

Item contribution margin

Item contribution margin category

Menu item classification

Menu mix percentage

Menu mix percentage popularity rate

Menu selling price

Miller matrix

Plow horse

Popularity index

Popular seller

Puzzle

Sales mix analysis

Sales volume percentage

Star

Total item contribution margin

Total item food cost

Total item revenue

Total menu contribution margin

Total menu food cost

Total menu revenue

Unpopular seller

Introduction

After a restaurant has been in operation, it is useful to determine the success of the menu in meeting the established target profit margins and the expectations of the target market. This chapter illustrates menu engineering. It also explains the purposes for menu sales mix analysis, how to perform one, how to change the menu based on the results of the analysis, and other uses of the results of the menu sales mix analysis.

Purposes of a Sales Mix Analysis

A **sales mix analysis** is an analysis of the popularity and the profitability for a group of menu items. One of the major purposes for performing a menu sales mix analysis is to monitor the effectiveness of the menu items to maximize profits. To effectively do this, the analysis should be done at least four times per year. The results of the menu sales mix analysis help determine whether changes in menu pricing, content, or design are needed.

The analysis includes determining which menu items are most popular and which contribute the most money to expenses and profit. (See *Exhibit 7a*.) It involves comparing menu items in terms of sales and profitability. Because profitability in this case is based on contribution margin or gross profit, the contribution margin for each item is determined.

Another purpose for the menu sales mix analysis is to determine which items have the highest sales. The menu sales for each item are compared so the manager or chef can determine which items sell most effectively.

The information gathered about which menu items sell the best affects certain aspects of purchasing. If the popularity index of a menu item is found to be high in relation to other menu items, then the purchaser will buy more of the ingredients of the popular menu item. In fact, the popularity index is often used to purchase products for a particular time period based on sales forecasts for the same time period.

Exhibit 7a

Entrée Popularity Bar Chart

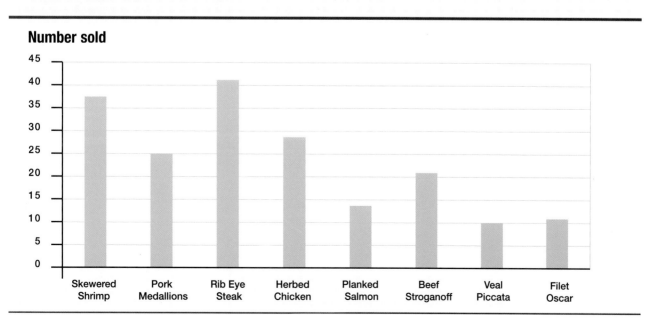

Number sold

Planning for the production of the menu items also depends on the popularity of each item. The kitchen manager or chef ensures that sufficient staff are on hand to produce the predicted menu items, and directs employees to pre-prep more of the popular items (in terms of sales volume) than the unpopular ones.

Another use of the information gathered about menu item sales and profitability includes evaluation of the menu item production processes. Some menu items are very labor-intensive and may require extra work or extra staffing to produce them, thus resulting in a higher than average labor cost for those menu items. The labor costs for the production of the individual menu items should be considered when decisions are made about the popularity and profitability of the items, as high labor costs will reduce the actual profitability of a menu item.

Activity

Part One: Labor Costs

Sally, an assistant restaurant manager, has been asked to evaluate the relative labor costs involved with producing two of the items on the menu. Both of the menu items are very popular and sales are high. They have very similar contribution margins. However, the manager thinks one of the items may require significantly more labor than the other. He is concerned that this extra labor may affect the real costs of production and reduce the amount of money that is used to provide profit and cover expenses. The two preparations are described below.

■ Rib Eye Steak requires little in the way of kitchen handling. It is taken from the refrigerated space beneath the counter and broiled. Then an order of fresh onion rings is breaded, deep-fried, and added to the plate with the steak for service.

■ Sweet and Sour Pork is made with pork that has to be cubed. Fried rice is prepared using small amounts of chopped garlic and onion. The rice is stir-fried with egg, peas, and bamboo shoots. Then the green peppers, tomatoes and pineapple chunks are cleaned and cut into bite-sized pieces. The pork is coated with a light batter and deep-fried. Then the sweet and sour sauce is made and combined with the green pepper, tomato, and pineapple, which have been stir-fried. The sauce is thickened, the pork is added, and when it is up to temperature, the mixture is put on top of the fried rice for service.

1 **What should Sally report to her manager?**

_____

_____

2 **What ideas do you have for helping to reduce the labor costs?**

_____

_____

Performing a Sales Mix Analysis

There are several steps to performing a sales mix analysis for a group of menu items.

1 Select items to compare.

2 Determine menu mix percentage popularity.

3 Determine menu item contribution margins.

4 Calculate total food costs and total item revenues.

5 Compare to average contribution margin.

6 Classify menu items.

7 Evaluate day-part sales.

Each step will be explained in turn and an example will be provided. Then you will practice what you have learned in an exercise.

The sales mix analysis is usually done using a format similar to *Exhibit 7b* on the next page. The subsequent examples and exercises in this chapter are coded to match the columns in *Exhibit 7b*.

Step 1: Select Items to Compare

Usually, a menu sales mix analysis method works best when it is done within a single menu category, not on the entire menu. This is because of the difficulty of comparing lists of different lengths and radically different sales volumes. For example, most customers usually buy an entrée, but less than half of customers purchase an appetizer. Therefore, it would be difficult to compare the menu mix percentage of entrées with the menu mix percentage of appetizers.

The first step is to list the menu items to be analyzed in the first column of the worksheet. In the example used in this chapter, the items in the entrée category will be analyzed, so all the entrées are listed in the *Menu Item* column (Column A) of *Exhibit 7b*.

Exhibit 7b provides you with the results of a complete sales mix analysis. In the following pages, each step in the analysis will be explained, as well as the calculations that are required for each step. The corresponding columns for the calculation of each step are provided along with an explanation of the step.

Exhibit 7b

Menu Engineering Worksheet

The Galleon   **June 1, 2006**

A Menu Item	B Number Sold	C Menu Mix % (B÷ΣB)	D Selling Price	E Item Food Cost	F Item Contribution Margin (D−E)
Skewered Shrimp	37	19.6	$12.95	$4.51	$ 8.44
Pork Medallions	25	13.3	15.50	5.71	9.79
Rib Eye Steak	42	22.2	14.95	5.38	9.57
Herbed Chicken	29	15.3	12.95	3.37	9.58
Planked Salmon	14	7.4	15.95	5.90	10.05
Beef Stroganoff	21	11.1	11.50	4.18	7.32
Veal Piccata	10	5.3	13.50	7.15	6.35
Filet Oscar	11	5.8	15.95	7.82	8.13
Totals	**189**				

Meal Period—Month of May

G Total Revenue (B×D)	H Total Food Cost (B×E)	I Total Item Contribution Margin (G−H)	J Contribution Margin Category (high or low)	K MM% Category (high or low)	L Menu Item Classification (dog, plow horse, puzzle, or star)
$ 479.15	$166.87	$ 312.28	Low	High	Plow horse
387.50	142.75	244.75	High	High	Star
627.90	225.96	401.94	High	High	Star
375.55	97.73	277.82	High	High	Star
223.30	82.60	140.70	High	Low	Puzzle
241.50	87.78	153.72	Low	High	Plow horse
135.00	71.50	63.50	Low	Low	Dog
175.45	86.02	89.43	Low	Low	Dog
$2,645.35	$961.21	$1,684.14			

Step 2: Determine Menu Mix Percentage Popularity

In the *Number Sold* column (Column B), list the numbers of each entrée sold in the analysis time period. Then, calculate the total number of entrées sold by adding all of the individual sales. Once the total number of entrées sold has been determined, calculate the **menu mix percentage**—also known as **popularity index** or **sales volume percentage**—of each entrée by dividing the number of specific items sold by the total number of items sold.

$$\frac{\text{Number of item sold}}{\text{Total number of all items sold}} = \text{Menu mix percentage of item}$$

The menu mix percentage (abbreviated MM%) for each item is then recorded in Column C.

The menu mix percentage popularity rate is determined next. The authors of the menu engineering concept, Kasavana and Smith, established that an item was considered a popular seller if its menu mix percentage was at least 70 percent of the expected average sales of the item. Michael Kasavana and Donald Smith calculate the **menu mix percentage popularity rate** by dividing 100 by the number of menu items being evaluated and then multiplying that number by seventy percent.

$$\left(100 \div \text{Number menu items}\right) \times 70\% = \text{Menu mix percentage popularity rate}$$

$$(100 \div 8) \times 0.70 = 8.75$$

The example in this chapter has eight menu items listed. Therefore, the menu mix percentage popularity rate (abbreviated MM% popularity rate) is 8.75 percent.

Next, the MM% of each of the menu items is compared to the MM% popularity rate to establish whether it is considered popular or unpopular.

- Items with an MM% at or above the MM% popularity rate are considered **popular sellers.**

- Items with an MM% below the MM% popularity rate are considered **unpopular seller.**

If an item is considered popular, the term "High" is recorded in the *MM% Category* (Column K). If an item is considered unpopular, then the term "Low" is recorded in Column K.

Menu Mix Percentage Category Results

A Menu Item	B Number Sold	C Menu Mix % (B÷ΣB)	K MM% Category (high or low)
Skewered Shrimp	37	19.6	High
Pork Medallions	25	13.3	High
Rib Eye Steak	42	22.2	High
Herbed Chicken	29	15.3	High
Planked Salmon	14	7.4	Low
Beef Stroganoff	21	11.1	High
Veal Piccata	10	5.3	Low
Filet Oscar	11	5.8	Low

In our example, the MM% of Skewered Shrimp is 19.6 percent. This is significantly higher than the MM% popularity rate of 8.75 percent, so the popularity of Skewered Shrimp is high. The *Menu Mix Percentage Category* (abbreviated *MM% Category*) of each of the items in the example is shown at left.

Activity

Part Two: Menu Item Popularity

Sally has been given the responsibility for determining the MM% of the menu items listed below. She must categorize each menu item in relation to its MM% category. She has been given the sales records from yesterday to make these determinations. Calculate the MM% and label the MM% category as either high or low based on your calculations.

A Menu Item	B Number Sold	C MM%	K MM% Category
Fried Chicken	375		
Porterhouse Steak	310		
Baked Halibut	110		
Beef Kabobs	70		
Roast Pork	135		
Total			

Menu Mix % Popularity Rate = _____

Step 3: Determine Menu Item Contribution Margins

The next step of the menu sales mix analysis is to determine each menu item's contribution margin. Start by listing the menu selling price of each of the entrées being evaluated in the *Selling Price* column (Column D). The menu selling price—the standard selling price, not a discounted price—for each item is found on the menu. Next, list the food cost of each item in Column E.

The item contribution margin for each item is the difference between the item's food cost and its menu selling price. This also is called the item's gross profit.

Item selling price − Item food cost = Item contribution margin

The contribution margin of each item is listed in Column F. The total item contribution margin for each menu item can be determined by multiplying the number of the menu items sold (Column B) by the contribution margin for the item (Column F).

$$\text{Number of item sold} \quad \times \quad \text{Item contribution margin} \quad = \quad \text{Total item contribution margin}$$

The total contribution margin for each item in our example is listed on pp. 140–141 in Column I. The total menu contribution margin is the sum of all the items' total item contribution margins.

Item Contribution Margin Results

A Menu Item	B Number Sold	D Selling Price	E Item Food Cost	F Item Contribution Margin	I Total Item Contribution Margin
Skewered Shrimp	37	$12.95	$4.51	$8.44	$312.28
Pork Medallions	25	15.50	5.71	9.79	244.75
Rib Eye Steak	42	14.95	5.38	9.57	401.94
Herbed Chicken	29	12.95	3.37	9.58	277.82
Planked Salmon	14	15.95	5.90	10.05	140.70
Beef Stroganoff	21	11.50	4.18	7.32	153.72
Veal Piccata	10	13.50	7.15	6.35	63.50
Filet Oscar	11	15.95	7.82	8.13	89.43
Totals	**189**				**$1,684.14**

Activity

Part Three: Menu Item Contribution Margin

Sally has been given the menu prices of the entrées, the current food cost of each menu item, and the sales records from yesterday. Find the contribution margin of each menu item and the total contribution margin for each of the menu items.

A	B	D	E	F	I
Menu Item	Number Sold	Selling Price	Item Food Cost	Item Contribution Margin	Total Item Contribution Margin
Fried Chicken	375	$10.50	$5.15		
Porterhouse Steak	310	16.45	8.50		
Baked Halibut	110	15.95	7.27		
Beef Kabobs	70	9.95	4.16		
Roast Pork	135	13.50	5.10		
Total					

Calculations:

Step 4: Calculate the Total Menu Contribution Margin by the Total Menu Method

An alternative way to determine the total menu contribution margin (gross profit) is to determine the total revenue of all the menu items and the total food costs of all the menu items, and then calculate the difference between them. We will call this the total menu method.

The **total item revenue** is found by multiplying the number of each item sold (Column B) by each item's menu selling price (Column D). The result is entered into the *Total Item Revenue* column (Column G).

Number sold × Menu price = Total item revenue

The total item revenues for each menu item (Column G) are then added together to find the **total menu revenue.**

To find the **total item food cost** (Column H) of the menu, multiply the number of each item sold (Column B) by each item's food cost (Column E).

Number sold × Item food cost = Total item food cost

The total item food costs for all items are then added together to find the **total menu food cost** (Column H).

Total Item Food Cost Results

A	B	D	E	G	H
Menu Item	Number Sold	Selling Price	Item Food Cost	Total Revenue (B×D)	Total Food Cost (B×E)
Skewered Shrimp	37	$12.95	$4.51	$479.15	$166.87
Pork Medallions	25	15.50	5.71	387.50	142.75
Rib Eye Steak	42	14.95	5.38	627.90	225.96
Herbed Chicken	29	12.95	3.37	375.55	97.73
Planked Salmon	14	15.95	5.90	223.30	82.60
Beef Stroganoff	21	11.50	4.18	241.50	87.78
Veal Piccata	10	13.50	7.15	135.00	71.50
Filet Oscar	11	15.95	7.82	175.45	86.02
Totals	**189**			**$2,645.35**	**$961.21**

Finally, calculate the **total menu contribution margin** by subtracting the total food cost (Column H) from the total menu revenue (Column G). This serves as a check on the former method of finding each item's contribution margin.

Total menu revenue   −   Total food cost   =   Total menu contribution margin

For example, the total menu contribution margin is determined by subtracting $961.21 from $2,645.35. This result is $1,684.14, which agrees with the total menu contribution margin determined by the combination of the first and second methods.

Activity

Part Four: Total Menu Contribution Margin

Sally's boss has asked her to verify the profitability of the menu by the total menu method. Calculate the total menu contribution margin for the following menu.

A	B	D	E	F	G	H
Menu Item	Number Sold	Selling Price	Item Food Cost	Item Contribution Margin	Total Revenue	Total Food Cost
Fried Chicken	375	$10.50	$5.15			
Porterhouse Steak	310	16.45	8.50			
Baked Halibut	110	15.95	7.27			
Beef Kabobs	70	9.95	4.16			
Roast Pork	135	13.50	5.10			
Total						

Total Menu Contribution Margin = _____

Step 5: Compare to Average Contribution Margin

Once the total contribution margin for each item has been obtained, each menu item can be compared to the **average contribution margin** Item. The average contribution margin is determined by dividing the total item contribution margin (the total in Column I) by the total number of menu items sold (the total in Column B).

$$\text{Total item contribution margin} \div \text{Total number of items sold} = \text{Average contribution margin}$$

In this case, $1,684.14 is divided by 189. The resulting number of $8.91 represents the average contribution margin per menu item.

Item Contribution Margin Results

A	B	F	I	J
Menu Item	Number Sold	Item Contribution Margin (D−E)	Total Item Contribution Margin (G−H)	Contribution Margin Category (high or low)
Skewered Shrimp	37	$8.44	$ 312.28	Low
Pork Medallions	25	9.79	244.75	High
Rib Eye Steak	42	9.57	401.94	High
Herbed Chicken	29	9.58	277.82	High
Planked Salmon	14	10.05	140.70	High
Beef Stroganoff	21	7.32	153.72	Low
Veal Piccata	10	6.35	63.50	Low
Filet Oscar	11	8.13	89.43	Low
Totals	**189**		**$1,684.14**	

Next, the contribution margin of each menu item can be compared to the average contribution margin to determine whether it is higher or lower than the average. If the item's contribution margin is higher than the average, then "High" is recorded in the **item contribution margin category** (Column J). If the item's contribution is lower than the average, then "Low" is recorded in Column J. In the example, the contribution margin of $8.44 for Skewered Shrimp is lower than the average contribution margin of $8.91. Therefore, it is considered low in regards to contribution margin and a "Low" appears in Column J.

Activity

Part Five: Menu Item Profitability Category

Sally had determined the contribution margin for each menu item she was evaluating. She knew the average contribution margin was found by dividing the total item contribution margin by the number of menu items sold. Find the average contribution margin and determine if each menu item's contribution margin is higher or lower than the average contribution margin.

Note: You will need to use the item contribution margins you calculated in Part Four of this activity.

A	B	F	I	J
Menu Item	Number Sold	Item Contribution Margin	Total Item Margin Contribution	Contribution Margin Category
Fried Chicken	375			
Porterhouse Steak	310			
Baked Halibut	110			
Beef Kabobs	70			
Roast Pork	135			
Total				

Average Contribution Margin = _____

Menu Item Classification

Star
CM: High
MM%: High

Plowhorse
CM: Low
MM%: High

Puzzle
CM: High
MM%: Low

Dog
CM: Low
MM%: Low

Step 6: Classify Menu Items

The next step in the menu sales mix analysis is to classify the menu items based on a combination of their MM% popularity rate category and their contribution margin category. The **menu item classification** scheme is shown in *Exhibit 7c.*

- If an item has a high MM% and a high contribution margin, it is classified as a star.

- If an item has a high MM% and a low contribution margin, it is classified as a plow horse.

- If an item has a low MM% and a high contribution margin, it is classified as a puzzle.

- If an item has a low MM% and a low contribution margin, it is classified as a dog.

Since the actions taken in regards to menu items is based on these classifications, it is important to assign a classification to each menu item. The results of assigning menu item classifications to our example are shown below.

Besides simply classifying the menu items in one of the four categories, their actual contribution margins and menu mix percentages can be plotted on a graph such as that shown in *Exhibit 7d.* Doing this shows which menu items are extremely good or bad—those at the edges of the graph—and which ones are just a little good or bad—those near the center. The menu items at the extremes should be treated soon; the ones near the middle can wait a little while because their effects are not that large.

Menu Item Classification Results

A	J	K	L
Menu Item	**Contribution Margin Category (high or low)**	**MM% Category (high or low)**	**Menu Item Classification (dog, plow horse, puzzle, or star)**
Skewered Shrimp	Low	High	Plow horse
Pork Medallions	High	High	Star
Rib Eye Steak	High	High	Star
Herbed Chicken	High	High	Star
Planked Salmon	High	Low	Puzzle
Beef Stroganoff	Low	High	Plow horse
Veal Piccata	Low	Low	Dog
Filet Oscar	Low	Low	Dog

Exhibit 7d

Contribution Margin/MM% Graph

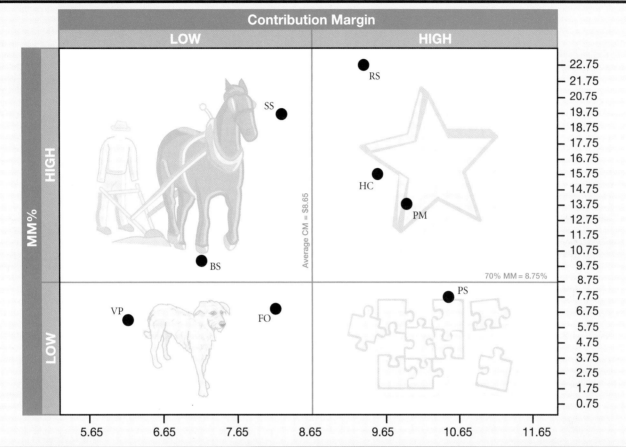

A	B	C	F
Menu Item	**Graph Code**	**MM%**	**Item Contribution Margin**
Skewered Shrimp	SS	19.60%	$ 8.44
Pork Medallions	PM	13.30	9.79
Rib Eye Steak	RS	22.20	9.57
Herbed Chicken	HC	15.30	9.58
Planked Salmon	PS	7.40	10.05
Beef Stroganoff	BS	11.10	7.32
Veal Piccata	VP	5.30	6.35
Filet Oscar	FO	5.80	8.13
Totals		**100.00**	**$69.23**
70% MM		**8.75%**	
Average CM			**$ 8.65**

Step 7: Evaluate Day-Part Sales

Another way to use sales mix analysis is to use it on day-part sales. Perhaps certain items are sold at a different price at lunch than at dinner. The impact this price difference has on the contribution margin and menu mix popularity can now be determined separately for each day part. Day-part sales were examined in the last chapter by using the individual sales analysis tools. Now the profitability and popularity can be evaluated using a combined method. The next section will describe some ways the menu items can be marketed to increase sales or profitability.

Changing the Menu Based on Analysis

The purpose for finding each menu item's popularity and profitability is to determine better how to merchandise the menu items on the physical menu to increase profitability. There are a variety of suggestions for what a menu planner might do with a menu item, but it is important to make any changes in the context of the brand image, the competitive market, the kitchen dynamic, the overall price category, and customer expectations.

The Stars

The menu items in the **star** category have been found to be highly profitable to the operation and very popular with the customers; these items may include the operations' signature items. Strategies to use for this category of menu item include:

- Do nothing, as they already sell well and make money for the operation.

- Ensure that these menu items are very visible on the menu in terms of layout and design.

- Maintain the specifications for the item including purchase, presentation, portion size, and quality.

- If these items are difficult for the customer to compare with the competition, try a price increase to determine the impact on menu mix. If the price increase is accepted, the total profitability increases for these items while the sales remain comparable.

- Promote them even more aggressively by the use of table tents and suggestive selling.

The Plow Horses

The menu items in the **plow horse** category are the menu items that sell very well but are not so profitable to the operation. They may be the items that bring in customers. However, selling a lot of them and not making much profit from them requires that they be examined for some change. Things to consider include:

- Pricing psychology could be used to increase the price to increase profitability. However, if these are very popular sellers and one of the reasons for their high sales is the price, this could reduce their sales.

- If they are very large portions, they could be reduced a little to decrease the food cost, thus increasing the contribution margin.

- If observation of the menu design indicates that they are presented in a very high-profile position on the menu, they could be moved to a less obvious spot on the menu.

- These items could be combined with another menu item that has a much lower food cost to increase the profitability of the new combined item.

- If a very close examination of the labor involved in producing these items shows that they are very labor-intensive, they could be removed from the menu or ways could be found to reduce the labor cost; for example, the ingredients required to produce the item could be purchased ready to use.

The Puzzles

The menu items in the **puzzle** category are the menu items that are very profitable to the operation, but not many of them are sold. Different changes you could make include:

- Customers may have perceived that these items did not provide the price-value relationship they were looking for, so reducing the price moderately may increase sales.

- The merchandising of these items could be increased by:
  - ☐ Moving these items to a more prominent position on the menu
  - ☐ Using table tents
  - ☐ Suggestive selling the items by waitstaff

- If the menu item has an unfamiliar name, it could be renamed to increase recognition and thus sales.

- If it is truly a puzzle, impacts the kitchen negatively because it is not prepared often, and does not help the restaurant image, it could be removed from the menu.

The Dogs

The menu items in the **dog** category have earned this classification because they are not profitable, and they do not sell well. Things to do with these menu items include:

- **Remove them from the menu.** If these items use inventory items not used in any other menu item or cause disruption in kitchen production, their removal from the menu will increase efficiency and reduce operationing costs.

- **Raise the price or reduce the cost of ingredients.** This will increase their profitability when they are sold; however, this action may reduce sales even further.

- **Reposition on menu.** The item could be hidden on the menu in a very low profile position and therefore might benefit from a change in placement on the menu.

- **Replace with an alternative menu item.** Of course, any menu item that is added should support the brand image and be tested within the operation before it is added to the menu.

Other Menu Sales Mix Analysis Methods

Two other sales mix analysis methods that use similar methodology to menu engineering are useful to consider. The **Miller matrix** attempts to identify menu items that are low in food cost and popular. In a Miller matrix analysis, the items on the menu are placed into four categories:

- Low in food cost and popular

- High in food cost and popular

- Low in food cost and unpopular

- High in food cost and unpopular

The low food cost/popular menu items were named winners and treated similarly to stars. In this analysis method, the best sales mix would result in sixty percent of the menu items sold in the low food cost category. This method is more useful in quick-service and low-average check operations.

The **cost-margin analysis** introduced by David Pavesic, well-known restaurant author, combines the food costs from the Miller matrix and the contribution margin concept from menu engineering. The contribution margins are weighted by sales (total contribution margin) and compared to food costs. Therefore, this methodology combines sales volume or popularity, food cost, and contribution margin. There are four basic steps to this method:

1 The food cost cut off is defined as the total weighted food cost of all menu sales.

2 This percentage is used as the standard against which individual menu items are measured to determine whether they were considered high or low in food cost.

3 The total weighted contribution margin is divided by the number of menu items being examined to determine the cut-off for high or low contribution margins.

4 Then each menu item is categorized into one of four categories:

☐ Low cost and high contribution margin

☐ Low cost and low contribution margin

☐ High cost and high contribution margin

☐ High cost and low contribution margin

In this method, the low cost and high contribution margin items are named Primes and are treated similarly to stars. An examination of the categories into which each menu item falls indicate possible actions to take in regard to marketing the menu items.

Activity

Part Six: Menu Changes

Sally has examined all the data about the menu items as requested by her manager. She has classified the menu items in terms of their profitability and popularity.

Now, the manager wants some suggestions from her on how to increase the profitability of the restaurant. What should be done with each of the menu items?

A	J	K	L
Menu Item	Contribution Margin Category	Menu Mix % Category	Menu Item Classification
Fried Chicken			
Porterhouse Steak			
Baked Halibut			
Beef Kabobs			
Roast Pork			

continued on next page

Part Six: Menu Changes *continued from previous page*

1   What does Sally have to consider before making any changes?

_____

_____

_____

_____

_____

_____

2 What could be done with these items based on their classifications?

A. Fried Chicken _____

B. Porterhouse Steak _____

C. Baked Halibut _____

D. Beef Kabobs _____

E. Roast Pork _____

Summary

A sales mix analysis analyzes the popularity and the profitability of a group of menu items. One of the major purposes for performing a menu sales mix analysis is to monitor the effectiveness of the menu items to maximize profits. Another purpose is to determine which items have the highest sales.

There are seven steps to performing a sales mix analysis. The first step is to select items on the menu to be compared in the analysis. The most accurate analysis will focus on one menu category, not on the entire menu. The next step is to determine the menu mix percentage (MM%), also known as the popularity index or sales volume percentage, of each item by dividing the number of specific items sold by the total number of items sold.

The third step is to determine the menu item contribution margin or gross profit, which is the difference between the item's food cost and it's menu selling price. After finding the individual item contribution margin, the total item contribution for each menu item can be found by multiplying the number of the menu items sold by the contribution margin for the item. An alternative method for calculating the total menu contribution margin is to determine the total revenue of all menu items and the total food costs of all the menu items, and calculating the differences between them.

Once the total contribution margin for each item has been determined, each menu item can be compared to the average contribution margin, or the total contribution margin divided by the total number of items sold. Whether or not the item's contribution margin falls above or below the average determines if it considered high or low.

The next step in the menu sales mix analysis is to classify the menu items as either stars, plow horses, puzzles, or dogs. Classifications are made by looking at the menu mix percentage and the contribution margin for each item. Decisions concerning a menu item's profitability can be made once items are classified into these categories.

There are alternative ways of doing a sales mix analysis, including the Miller Matrix, which is more useful in quick-service and low average check operations, and the cost-margin analysis, which combines the food costs from the Miller Matrix and the contribution margin concept from menu engineering.

Review Your Learning

1 **How is the contribution margin of a menu item found?**

A. By subtracting the menu-selling price from the food cost

B. By subtracting the cost of food from the menu-selling price

C. By multiplying the number sold by the menu price

D. By multiplying the number sold by the sales volume

2 **The menu mix percentage is found by**

A. dividing the number of each menu item sold by the total menu items sold.

B. dividing the contribution margin by the total menu items sold.

C. subtracting the contribution margin from the food cost.

D. subtracting the contribution margin from the menu-selling price.

3 **Menu items are classified as puzzles if they have a**

A. high MM% and a high contribution margin.

B. high MM% and a low contribution margin.

C. low MM% and a high contribution margin.

D. low MM% and a low contribution margin.

4 **Which of the following is *not* considered when changing a menu?**

A. Other restaurants in the area

B. Customers' expectations

C. Previous chef's favorite item

D. Brand image of the operation

5 **If a menu item is classified as a star, you should**

A. take it off the menu.

B. reduce the price.

C. combine it with an item with a lower food cost.

D. do nothing.

6 **Labor intensive items**

A. use up more of the contribution margin than an item that is not labor intensive.

B. should all be removed from the menu no matter what.

C. should be sent to the restaurant across the street for preparation.

D. use up more food costs than an item that is not labor intensive.

7 **Once the restaurant is in operation, how often should a menu sales mix analysis be performed?**

A. Once, to be sure the menu is working

B. Daily, for the best and most cost-effective results

C. Approximately four times per year

D. Whenever the manager can do it

8 **The average contribution margin is found by dividing the**

A. total contribution margin by the number of items being evaluated.

B. total contribution margin by the total number of menu items sold.

C. food cost by the menu selling price.

D. menu selling price by the food cost.

Field Project

Financial Procedures Audit

This field project will provide you with an opportunity to learn from practitioners in the restaurant industry and find out how the concepts that have been covered in this competency guide are used in actual practice. Because menus are central to restaurant operation, this practicum is designed to give you an in-depth look at how a particular restaurant manages its menu.

Assignment

Find a restaurant that sells food and alcoholic beverages, in which you can spend fifteen to twenty hours learning how the menu contributes to the restaurant's success. To do this, you must get permission from the restaurant manager to observe its operations and ask questions. These questions will be about the menu's development, including item selection, layout and design, pricing strategies, sales analysis, and the impact of beverage sales.

Note: If you are younger than twenty-one, you may be excused from the part of the practicum concerning alcoholic beverages. You should arrange to be at the restaurant when alcoholic beverages are not served; for example, during the hours between the lunch and dinner shifts.

Upon completion of the fifteen to twenty hours, write an in-depth report discussing your findings. You must also describe five recommendations that you would suggest to the manager based on your findings. Include a copy of the menu with your report, along with any other menu-related tools that can be gathered from the restaurant, such as a daily sales report, table tents merchandising food or beverage items, nutritional information handouts, and so forth.

Include in Your Report

1 A description of the restaurant:

☐ Where is it located?

☐ Does it have a logo or brand?

☐ What is the décor like?

☐ Who are the customers that the restaurant serves, in terms of target market?

☐ How large is the restaurant (number of seats in the dining room, etc.)?

☐ What kind of storage space does the restaurant have?

☐ What types of equipment are used to prepare food?

☐ How is food prepared—from scratch, or from convenience food?

☐ How many items does the restaurant carry in its inventory?

2 A description of the menu or menus used:

☐ What meals are served?

☐ Are there any special menus, such as a children's menu, dessert menu, or wine list?

☐ What courses are served (appetizers, side items, entrées, salads, desserts, etc.)?

☐ What kinds of food are offered? Is there a variety? Any health-conscious items?

Include in Your Report *continued from previous page*

☐ What kinds of alcoholic beverages are sold? Is there a variety? How many choices of wine, beer, and hard liquor?

☐ What food preparation methods are used to prepare the food as indicated on the menu (grilling, broiling, frying, etc.)?

☐ What items are located at the menu's focus points?

☐ Does the menu identify specials or direct the customer's attention to any particular items?

☐ What is the price point or price category, according to your examination of the menu?

☐ Is the menu easy to read? Would elderly customers find it easy to read?

☐ Does the menu help support the décor?

☐ What other observations can be made about the physical appearance of the menu (colors used, type of material, how many pages, etc.)?

3 A discussion of pricing:

☐ What is the average check per person for each meal?

☐ How are food and beverage costs identified?

☐ How are food and beverage prices determined?

☐ What percentage of sales is created by food sales? Beverage sales?

☐ How often are prices changed? What influences a price change?

4 Sales analysis information:

☐ What information is kept about sales?

☐ What types of sales analysis are done? By whom? What changes in the menu have resulted from sales analysis?

☐ How are new menu items introduced? How often are new menu items added?

☐ What are the sales trends?

5 Manager's analysis:

☐ Which restaurant(s) does the manager view as competition?

☐ What industry trends can the manager identify?

☐ What are the strengths and weaknesses of the operation?

☐ What customer trends has the manager noticed?

6 Observations:

☐ Describe the overall ambience of the restaurant.

☐ Describe the type of service provided to customers.

☐ Was the manager helpful in answering your questions?

☐ What actual practices did you find that support or do not support what you have learned in this competency guide?

7 Recommendations:

☐ List five recommendations you would make to the manager about the menu, pricing, sales analysis, food production, etc., based on your research.

Report Grading Guidelines

A complete report will include the following items (items marked with a * are particularly important):

1 Restaurant Description

- ☐ Location
- ☐ Description of logo or brand
- ☐ Description of décor
- ☐ Target market, customers
- ☐ Restaurant size, number of seats
- ☐ Storage space
- ☐ Kitchen equipment
- ☐ Food preparation: From scratch, or from convenience foods?
- ☐ Size of inventory

2 Menu Description

- ☐ Meals served
- ☐ Special menus (children's menu, dessert menu, wine list, etc.)
- ☐ Courses included in each meal (appetizers, side items, entrées, salads, desserts, etc.)
- ☐ Foods offered: Is there a variety? Any health-conscious items?
- ☐ Alcoholic beverages offered: What types? Is there a variety within each type?
- ☐ Food preparation methods used, as indicated on menu
- ☐ Menu specials—is the customer's attention directed to particular items?
- ☐ Price point or price category identified, based on menu observation
- ☐ Description of menu readability
- ☐ Does the menu support the décor? How?
- ☐ Description of physical menu (colors used, type of material, how many pages, etc.)

3 Pricing Discussion

- ☐ * Average check for each meal
- ☐ Identification of method used to find food and beverage costs
- ☐ * Complete explanation of how food and beverage prices are determined
- ☐ Percentage of sales created by food; by beverages
- ☐ * Price changes: How often? What influences the changes?

4 Sales Analysis

- ☐ Explanation of sales records
- ☐ * Description of sales analysis methodology used: Who performs it? Does it result in change?
- ☐ New menu items: How are items introduced? How often?
- ☐ Sales trend information

Report Grading Guidelines *continued from previous page*

5 Manager's Analysis

☐ Competition for the restaurant as viewed by manager

☐ Discussion of industry and customer trends as identified by manager

☐ Compare strengths and weaknesses of operation as noted by manager

6 Observations

☐ Description of the restaurant ambience

☐ Description of service provided

☐ Helpfulness of manager

☐ * Compare actual practices observed in restaurant with topics covered in review guide

7 * Recommendations

☐ Includes five recommendations

☐ Recommendations are explained and based on student observation and interview with manager, and are supported by comments made earlier in report.

Index

Index